# Mafia Freedom

*An Offer I Couldn't Refuse*

TOMMY HAWK

Mafia Freedom: An Offer I Couldn't Refuse



ISBN-13: 978-1475249088

ISBN-10: 147524908X

# SPECIAL DEDICATION

## MOTHER

I know you have suffered greatly though the years. Two marriages down the drain, losing two sons and almost losing me to drugs or possible death from the Mafia. However, God has brought us both through it all. Your determination to make it through the years has influenced me greatly. Yes, God has brought us both through many years of brutal rejection.

You are now 92 and still counting. Through your praying, I am still alive and this book has become a reality. You have always been there for me Mother when almost everyone else rejected and cast me aside. If God had not kept me alive through your praying, and working His grace in me, this book would not be a reality. Your faithfulness in praying is helping hundreds of thousands throughout the globe.

Thank you for loving and encouraging me through the years. You are the only person on this earth who has always been there for me no matter the circumstances. Thank you for following me in your prayers as I traveled in country music and now as a bible teacher. I am glad to hear you say that the anointing has been powerful as you are praying for this book. There are no words to express my love and thanks to you Mother.

*I love you*!
Tommy

# CONTENTS

# ACKNOWLEDGMENTS

Apart from my own efforts, the success of this book depended on the encouragement of many others who heard me in person or read my story in a publication. I take this opportunity to express my gratitude to my friends who have been instrumental in rooting me on to the completion of this book:

Monvil Swain:
Best friend through my school years.

Ed Copeland:
My best friend in Cleveland through my drug years.

John Leto:
My best friend in Florida.

Byron Schwenn:
My Grace-friend in Columbus, Ohio

**Arkansas**
Joanie Thomas

**Columbus, Ohio**
Scott Kelso
Gary Larson
Scott & Jeanne Ferguson

Ray & Jan Frost
Murfreesboro, TN

## KARAOKE JOCKEYS

Richie KJ & DJ
Mike on the mike
Tom KJ
Patty KJ
Lin KJ

## PROOF READERS

Linda Van Fleet
Ed Copeland
Roy Nichols

## KARAOKE FRIENDS & SINGERS

Wayne
Dottie
Linda
Howie
Frankster
Goatster
Nicole
Ricky
Sammy
Dottie
Johnny
Howard
Patty
Jimmy
Angelina
Johnny
Ed

Dan & Memory
Glenn & Brenda
Bud & Roseann
Roy
Mary
Sammy
Bobbie
Wolf
Ron
Howard
Roland
Dave
Ramona
Pete
Ruthie
Stacy

# INTRODUCTION

He looked at me, laid a .38 revolver on the table, and asked, "Does the company owe you any money, Tommy?"

"No. Why do you ask?" I said nervously.

"If they do, we will make sure the president of the company hand delivers it to you." I will never forget the paternal look on Tony's face.

I was a very *successful* Country and Western recording artist until the *nightly* glory of the stage failed to provide satisfaction for *daily* living. I ended up a *successful* mess as the entertainer buzz faded.

My thoughts were, "I just need to make a lot of money to find satisfaction." I entered the business world in Columbus, Ohio, with Consumer Companies of America (CCA). I was well on my way to making $20,000 dollars per week as I was still trying to find some kind of fulfillment through money. However, the stress from long hours and building from the ground up was overwhelming.

The year 1976, was the pinnacle of my success. My position with CCA was Sales Director for West Virginia. My place of business was Charleston. As my connections to the Mafia grew, I accidentally found out that a large torch operation was head quartered there. A torch operation consists of professional fire arsonists who start fires for people who want to collect insurance money or have someone *whacked* in a fire.

My marriage was on the cocaine rocks, money meant nothing, and Mafia pressures were closing in on me like a lion stalking its prey. My secretary handed me a check for $3,000 [dollars] – my commission for the week – and if she had left my office at that moment, I would have fallen on my office floor and wept like a baby. Facing the abyss with thoughts of suicide filling my mind, I left the office determined to put an end to my misery. The only time my wife and I had any fun was when we were drinking, high on cocaine, or smoking dope. After years in the fast lane with big bucks, Learjet trips, cocaine addiction, and Mafia friends, my emotions were out of control, as I gained no satisfaction from my accomplishments. Nothing satisfied me, and I felt like a man stranded in a hot desert without water, chasing mirages. I was beginning to wonder what life was all about, since money still left me feeling miserable? With all the Mafia connections, money and success, where is the fulfillment?

My breakfast (and lunch) consisted of two lines of cocaine. In the evenings, for dinner, it was typically steak or lobster – and a late night snack, more cocaine. For the next thirty days, the money increased, along with the depression. My family had no idea of my inside turmoil. Suicide plagued my thoughts and controlled me as I reached the apex of my success, yet I was discouraged, depressed, and felt utterly hopeless. Suicide seemed to be the only way out from this depression.

The week when I was at my lowest, the president of the company called me and asked if I could get the company a loan from my mafia syndicate friends in Cleveland. Ten million dollars was the number back then, but today it would be around thirty million. Consumer Companies of America (CCA) was going bankrupt and now I had something to keep my mind off my misery.

While talking to *the people* about the loan, my most exciting and powerful time, was staying at a Celebrity Hotel in Cleveland. This was a party gathering place for celebrities of every profession and a meeting place for the Mafia. People like Frank Sinatra, The Rolling Stones, Muhammad Ali, President Jimmy Carter, Dean Martin and many more stayed there.

In the lobby, the smell of garlic and fresh-baked Italian bread would over power you and draw you into the restaurant. The male waiters were in first-class dress, including white gloves and black bowties. They were there to serve and to make your evening a first-class experience. After dinner, with garlic breath and spaghetti sauce on our lips, I accompanied Tony, Sammy, and Joey upstairs to my room to talk about the loan.

If you ask an Italian for help or a favor and they reply, "Yeah, we have some connections, we know *some people*," don't stick around to meet those *people*. Because of my ego and greed, I wanted to meet *the people*. By knowing "*the people,*" I loved the power I was gaining. This was a crucial step for me as I was walking ignorantly and blindly into bondage with the Cleveland Mob.

As we sat in my room, Sammy spoke, "Tommy, we will be taking over the company, and you will be the new president." Wow, *what an offer! Who could refuse?* Then he asked, "If we loan CCA ten million dollars, what are you going to use for security, your family?" I don't remember my thoughts, but I am sure the security of my family was not important. I think his question was more of a statement than asking a question. As this man continued to make demands, my friend, Tony, looked at me like a father. His eyes said, "Please do not do this, Tommy."

Tony had connections and knew many of *the people* and everyone loved him. He never became a big wheel in the Mafia because he could not hurt anyone. He managed me in the country music business for many years. He was a partner in a major talent agency in California that booked major Hollywood stars such as one of his best friends, Phyllis Diller. He was extremely close to the Sinatra family, and worked for MGM Records for 20 years and had a major influence in the release of the song *Spiders and Snakes*, by Jim Stafford. For you old timers, he also managed "*The Poni-Tails*" singing group.

We took a trip to Philadelphia to meet the talk show host Mike Douglas and while Tony was in the bathroom, I was alone with Mike. He said, "Tommy, Tony is loved throughout the entertainment industry." Mike went on to share how Tony spent three days with Elvis in Germany. Tony told me many stories about Elvis that have never been shared in a book or movie. Tony was ninety-eight when he passed away.

As my contacts increased with *the people*, I had many fascinating experiences. I conversed many times on the phone with a man from Lowell, Massachusetts. We discussed my Cleveland situation, and even though he had tried to lend me money, I would always say no, because I knew I would be in his control and be saddled with an excessive burden of interest.

I ended up meeting this man in South Florida a couple of years later. It was like playing a part in a Hollywood Mafia movie in real time. The camera is on and the producer says, "ACTION!" I picked him up at the airport; he took me to Hialeah Park Race Track to bet on the horses. As the camera pans in, he looks like a hit man with a face out of the movie "The Godfather." The next scene, we arrive at the racetrack. We walked up to a man who was smoking a cigar while leaning against a post. He motioned us over and gave us a horse to bet on. They were doing me a favor, and I wondered, "Will this give them the control they want over me?" What happened next left me shocked.

After my involvement with the Mafia, I ended up entangled in the destructive web of religion. My Christian religion bondage actually started out when I was a young man. I could not keep the religious rules and regulations of the church, so I ran from religion into Country Music and eventually developed Mafia connections. Trying to get free from Christian religion has been much more stressful and difficult than getting free from the grip of the Mafia. Many people today ask me, "What religion are you into?" My response: "I am not into religion."

Over the years, people asked me how I became so involved with the Mafia and how I escaped. I could not answer the questions simply or concisely, so this book is an attempt to provide the answers.

The story you are reading is true, but to protect anyone from embarrassment, names were changed or not mentioned.

# 1

# PHYSICAL, MENTAL, AND SPIRITUAL ABUSE

In the movie *The Godfather*, Don Corleone said, "A man, who doesn't spend time with his *family*, can never be a real man." In my opinion, the Corleone's seemed to have more compassion for *family* and people than do many people in organized rule-based religion. The emotional pain from family rejection and churches sent me searching for a *family* that would accept me, and that was a Mafia *family*.

My family grew up in the hills of Southern Ohio where the word Mafia did not exist. As far as immorality, mother and dad could have written the script for the immoral acts in *The Godfather* movie. "Your Cheating Heart," by Hank Williams, describes both of my parents. When mother was pregnant in the hospital, dad had an affair with Ruth, a family acquaintance. Mother found out about it and said, "Sooner or *later* I will get even." Well, *later* came many years *later*, I began to hear her talking on the phone with Pat. She spent many hours on the phone and somehow I knew she was going to see him.

One day, she left the house and started walking into the woods.

I yelled, *"Mom, where are you going?"*

She replied, *"You get back to the house."*

I went back to the house, knowing she was meeting Pat. After a few minutes, I made my way into the woods, hid behind a tree and witnessed the sexual act. I ran back to the house shocked, and I didn't know the damage until years later.

I don't remember mother ever saying anything good about dad. I didn't realize it at the time, but over the years, her bitterness influenced my attitude toward him. She hated him and I took up her offense, received her bitterness and resentment unknowingly. In her eyes, dad never did anything that was right or good. Her offense and bitterness became mine and helped destroy my relationship with him. Living around dad and hating him was worse than the hard work on a farm.

Our farming consisted of raising tobacco, tending a garden, and milking one cow. We had plenty to eat, because most of our food was harvested from the garden. In the winter, we had a good supply because Mother worked hard canning. Because of hunting season, September through the end of the year was my favorite time. When I was young, I was quite a hunter. I used to kill sixty or more squirrels a year plus many rabbits. I would love to have a big squirrel right now and fry it crispy like chicken. Our favorite part was the head and we all argued about who would get the head. There is very little meat but the brains are awesome. (Don't knock'em until you have tried'em!).

Eating out never was an option, except for grabbing a squirrel leg and going outside. Ha! Every now and then, we would go to the Shake Shoppe in Gallipolis, Ohio, for ice cream—but we seldom had that luxury. Working for farmers in the hay fields, tobacco patches, and cornfields for fifty cents per-hour provided money for a weekend of excitement—attending drive-in movies and playing pool in the billiard hall provided my entertainment. Playing pool became one of my ways of hustling money. That, unfortunately, was my excitement in the hills of Southern, Ohio as a young boy.

While growing up on the farm in Mercerville, I do not remember anyone in our family hugging or telling us kids, "We love you." My life was one of rejection, including mental and physical abuse. Adding to the pain, growing up on a tobacco farm was not easy, especially at eight or nine years old. Many times in the summer, I would work for fifty cents per hour in the fields for my grandfather on dad's side of the family. I would have to sleep over, because I was working a number of days at a time. There was only one place I could sleep, and that was upstairs with my uncle. He molested me many times, and the result of this was an ongoing battle for many years as I dealt with the sexual and emotional abuse.

Dad was a tyrant and he abused my whole family physically and mentally, with beatings and words like, "You will never amount to anything," or "You are not worth the salt in your bread." With mother's help, I grew to hate him with a passion, and at one point, I considered killing him while he was beating her. My father, uncle, and mother unknowingly did some serious emotional damage to me, and it has taken many years of struggling through *performance* trying to earn acceptance. The only acceptance I received from dad was, after ten hours of work on the farm, I would reach out for his acceptance and would say, "I am tired," and he would respond with, "A little hard work won't hurt you." I would perform for acceptance but he never once said, "You worked hard today and did a good job. I am proud of you." If you have kids, they need your affirmation more than they need the things you buy them. It is never too late to start hugging them.

Attending school as a young boy, the abuse continued because I was the one the bullies beat on. I found acceptance from my friend Monvil, but physical attacks from school mates continued through my preteen and teenage years. Going through school, the rejection was severe and each year it increased. I began to hate the ones who abused me as it continued day after day. Mother would always make sure we were clean and our hair combed neatly. As soon as I would get on the bus, Doug would make fun of me and always mess up my hair before I would get to school. Like with dad, I grew to hate him. As I write this, I can still see his look of disgust with me on his face. With the exception of Monvil, my hate and fear of rejection increased because of the kids making fun of my bib overalls. My parents were not able to buy me regular jeans, so I was stuck with bibs.

We had plenty to eat and our finances were just enough to get by. Our church taught that it was a sin to have money. If that were true, we were sinless. We were so poor we could not pay attention. We were so poor; we had to have a co-signer to pay cash. Ha! I ran from church people, as most of them were mean and unloving. I ran to *the people* who would accept me just as I was which included country music fans and, ultimately, *the Mafia*, whom I began to worship.

# 2

# LIFE IN COUNTRY MUSIC

Everything I knew about country music came from listening to the Grand Ole Opry on Saturday nights and dreaming of being a country singer. My mother, sister and I started singing in church and later my sister and I performed on the Buddy Starcher Television Show from Charleston, WV.

We lived on a farm so far back in the Southern Ohio woods, June bugs didn't get there until August. Getting out of the woods, off the farm and away from dad, was my youthful goal. The week I graduated from Hannan Trace High School, I moved to Columbus, Ohio. I left my *unloving* home, my siblings, and the tobacco farm in order to begin a new life in the big city.

My first job was flipping hamburgers at Sandy's fast food restaurant. My attitude stunk so bad, I lost that job and six others that same year. All my fears and past *rejection* destroyed all confidence in learning a new job. Because of fear, I could not take *correction* because, to me it was just more *rejection.* The fear continued for many years, going from job-to-job paved the road for me enter country music and the Mafia.

A few years later Roger, one of my younger brothers, died in an accident, and I launched my country music career to help deal with his death. I started performing at a local club, although the grief and emptiness from past years continued to haunt me.

Not knowing if I would ever find peace of mind, I decided to try the Nashville scene with the hope of getting some of my songs published and land a recording contract. I was also hoping the country music atmosphere of Nashville would soothe my emptiness. However, nothing changed. I rented a place close to Nashville's Music Row, only to suffer more rejection from all the publishers and record companies.

I was so craving recognition and acceptance; I started playing the bass guitar, and put my name on the bulletin board at the Ernest Tubb Record Shop for hire. I wanted in the country music limelight and was willing to do anything to get there. A few days later, Country Music Grand Ole Opry Star Kitty Wells, invited me to her house for an audition. I thought, "Oh wow, my big break." This was such an honor to be in the home of a legend. However, after a short time Kitty said, "Tommy, I am sorry but you do not have enough experience." She was very nice and right, but to me it was more rejection. I was so looking for acceptance; I shrugged it off and mumbled, "That was not what I was looking for anyway, I want to sing."

A few days later, I met Country music Star Penny Dehaven. She had many Top 40 Country hits in the early 1970's including her biggest hit "Land Mark Tavern" also a duet with Del Reeves in 1970. We dated but never hit it off. After my encounter with Kitty Wells, Penny Dehaven, and a year of failing to land a contract, I moved back to Columbus and formed my band, *"Tommy Hawk and His Warriors."* After performances throughout the United States and

Canada, I returned to Nashville and recorded my first album at the famous Bradley's Barn in Mt. Juliet. Many of the country stars recorded there like Conway Twitty, George Jones, and Loretta Lynn. My thoughts were, "Maybe this will satisfy this emptiness." It was so exciting to record in the same studio as Conway and others. Today, my most requested karaoke song is "Hello Darlin."

I was an invited guest on WSM Radio's Ralph Emery Show the day I released my first record "*I USED IT ALL ON YOU,*" and was I excited. The show precedes the Saturday Night Grand Ole Opry where he interviews the stars that have new releases. I cannot remember how I ended up on that show; however, I do remember I was on cloud *ten* with my first release.

My song was number one on WMNI Radio in Columbus and getting major airplay across the country. Many years later, my music tracks came up missing; however, you can Google the song and listen. I was close to becoming a major country star, but there was something still missing. My song was getting a lot of airplay in fifteen states and then another disaster: I ran out of money trying to keep the record in the shops, and as a result, it dropped off the charts.

I went back on the road again, only this time in a big bus and inscribed on the side "TOMMY HAWK AND HIS WARRIORS." On my last professional visit to Nashville, country music star Lori Morgan's Manager approached me and asked if I would take her on the road. At that time, Andrea traveled with me and in my opinion; she was a better singer than Lori. I declined and that was probably the biggest mistake I made while in Country music.

I traveled for many years and was so excited to be living my dream. I enjoyed the excitement of singing and performing many impersonations, including Kitty Wells, Johnny Cash, Johnny Carson, John Wayne, Whispering Bill Anderson, Walter Brennan, Buck Owens, and Meryl Haggard. I always enjoy doing Elvis, I still have my Elvis show suit to prove it, but it has shrunk—ha!

This all took a backseat to the loneliness. Traveling in a big bus, pulling into a Country Music Night Club and seeing my name in lights was my big buzz or ego trip for the day or a few hours. While performing, I felt accepted by applause from all the fans. After the show, alone in my hotel room, loneliness and depression would always show up overshadowing the evening attention. There was still something missing, but I kept performing for my *fix* night after night.

A short time later, adding to my emptiness and heartbreak, my other brother Freddie left this world through an airplane accident. When we were younger, we passed for twins. Many times the girls we were dating could not tell us apart until they got up close. If we were driving through Gallipolis, the only way you could tell us apart was by the color of our '57 Chevys; his was black and mine was candy apple red.

I met my future wife in the summer of 1973. Within a short time, she introduced me to some of her Mafia contacts. What impressed me about her was the willingness to use her contacts to help me succeed in the country music business, even if it meant endangering her. I will never forget her willingness to sacrifice. She captured my heart and a year later became my wife. I didn't know if I would ever enjoy a family because the doctors told her she would never be able to get pregnant and if she did, would never be able to deliver. You just didn't tell her that she couldn't do something because then she would break her neck trying. We were married in 1974, and while she was pregnant with our son, she traveled with me to my first underworld nightclub at the cape in Hyannis Port, Massachusetts. Shortly after giving birth to Shaun, then later came, Charity. I am so proud of my children and grandkids; they are the greatest.

Cape Cod was where I began to make further syndicate contacts and my first encounter with the Mob, where I could have been *whacked*. I was at the Office Bar where the boys hung out, and for some reason, I was left in charge one evening. There was a safe in the side room and while I wasn't looking, someone ripped it off. That evening *the people* came to me and said, "Tommy, if we thought you did this, you would be lying in the lake, so forget about it." I thought this was great, wow look with whom I am rubbing elbows! I now see how money, power, and getting my name up in lights at the Cape blinded me to what could have been certain death. However, my number one goal was to make it big in the country music world. I now had my chance. My ambitions led me around the country and into deeper involvement with the underworld. My contacts, flashy cars, and expensive clothes were nice, but something was still missing.

As the years passed, I performed at some of the most popular places throughout the United States and Canada; not realizing the next tour was my last.

We went to Thief River Falls, Minnesota, in the middle of the winter. My bus froze up and it was so cold, I saw a dog stuck to fire hydrant. Ha! If you had tried to walk a quarter mile you would have frozen to death. However, the bitter cold was worth it, because I was looking forward to "The Silver Saddle," an awesome club in Pueblo, Colorado, then to Grand Junction and finishing in Albuquerque, New Mexico.

After Grand Junction, CO, our next scheduled performance was the most popular place for country music stars in the United States at that time: "The Caravan East" in Albuquerque, New Mexico. This was the pinnacle of success for any country music singer who is trying to become a star. You really had to be a great performer and have a great traveling band to get booked there. It took me months of follow up calls and sending copies of our recordings to schedule this great club. I think the big reason I was accepted was, my first record, "*I Used It All on You*" played big time in those areas. Being able to perform at "The Caravan East" was like winning a country music award or being invited to perform at "The Grand Ole Opry." My band consisted of a fiddle, steel guitar, drummer, bass, and lead guitar. I also had great female singers that traveled with us. Shelby

Carter, the queen of Comanche County, OK, traveled with us on this tour.

We were about half way through our stay at "The Caravan East" and one day I was very aware that I was not feeling well. I was not sick, tired, or in any pain. At night, I was okay, but throughout the day, I felt so alone and empty. A mountain overlooks the city of Albuquerque for tourists, so I decided to drive up there and look around. It was a beautiful day as I focused on getting to the top of this mountain. When I arrived at the top, I was looking out over the city, and I knew something was going on inside of me. There was no physical pain, however, there was loneliness and emptiness that produced pain in my emotions that was more severe than body pain. I saw beautiful flowers all around me but could not focus on them. My thoughts were, "Am I depressed? I can't be depressed, I am Tommy Hawk; look at my headlines. I am traveling all over the country; my name is in lights, how could I be depressed? I am living my dream; however this is not what I expected. There is something missing that I can't put my finger on."

This lifestyle is what I had dreamed of, however, something was wrong and I was determined to find out what it was. With my eyes full of water and gazing over the city of Albuquerque, tears streaming down my cheeks, I wrote my wife a letter through the tears with a sincere message between the lines, country music has been the other woman and this is my last road trip. I know she probably said, "Yeah right."

# 3

# GETTING RICH IS THE ANSWER

After leaving Albuquerque in 1974 and returning to Columbus, I continued performing locally the rest of the year. On December 31, my manager, Tony, scheduled me to perform for Mayor Perk in Cleveland for the New Year's Eve Celebration. Thousands gathered as I sang, played the fiddle, and did my Elvis impersonation.

After this show was over, I was reminded once more of the emptiness that gnawed at me in Albuquerque. While I was performing, the applause covered the pain and numbed the emptiness. After that New Year's Eve, more thoughts of ending it all were controlling my thinking. There was just something missing, and I could not put my finger on it, even though I kept hearing some of my brother's last words about love: "I love you, you know that don't you?" I kept pushing those words down but they began to pierce my suicidal thinking. I was condescending in my thoughts and words toward Freddie because, to me, he was just a good ole boy, a truck driver and mechanic. I did notice the love he had for people and how many loved him. However, I just could not accept that anyone really loved me, including him.

Rejection hurts, and I was in a building a program, building a wall of protection around me. To hear someone say, "I love you" was foreign, and those words hindered the construction of my wall. If you are used to performing for acceptance and still never hear those words, as you know, the inner suffering is *indescribable.*

Money had to be what I was missing, so I sold my bus and set a goal to get rich. Every goal I had set I was always able to reach, except one, and that was filling the empty hole in the middle of my chest. I had always been good at sales, so I decided to go full blast into sales. I had been considering suicide but instead of attempting suicide, I figured that money had to be the answer that would fill this dark empty hole.

One night I was singing in Columbus when Don and Violet approached me with a question. "Tommy, do you want to get rich?" Well, this is where my head was, so I went to work for Consumer Companies of America (CCA) in Columbus, Ohio. After a couple of months with the company, I was one of the top ten producers and had set my first goal to get a new Lincoln Mark IV. I was making big money and within a few months, I bought my first of many new cars. I had my *fix.* I was satisfied, but I didn't know for how long. Within a few weeks, driving that new car was no different from any other *fix.* I ended up being a sales motivational speaker and trainer for the company. In my opinion, everyone is a sales person. I found that if you can get people sold on your company and product, it will breed excitement, and they can accomplish any financial goal.

This reminds me of a true story about Don that I always loved to share to make the point that you can accomplish any goal. Don was taking a short cut through a graveyard on his way home from the bar. He had taken this path for years and so tonight, he expected nothing out the ordinary. However, here is what he didn't know: the gravediggers had dug a fresh grave in his path that evening while he was at the bar. It was dark and raining and all of a sudden, he was at the bottom of this grave. He was cold, wet, and unsuccessful in accomplishing his goal of getting out of the grave. So he figured, "I will lie down, go to sleep and wait for the gravediggers tomorrow morning." All of a sudden, he hears footsteps and lo and behold, another man taking the same short cut falls in. Don was sitting in the other corner of the grave and he hears this man trying to get out. This second man does not know that Don was right there behind him. After a couple of seconds, Don is thinking to himself, "He can't get out of here, because I have already tried, so I will tell him." Don gets up and goes over to where he thinks he is standing and his hand touches the back of his neck, and he said to him, "You can't get out of here." But he did! That other man jumped out of that grave and accomplished his goal because he got motivated.

My *success* in Columbus was not enough to fill the hole and comfort my growing depression. I just had to make more money. Therefore, I set a goal to become financially independent. My thinking was, "If I could just get rich and play golf in all my spare time, then I would fill this hole inside of me." After many months in the Columbus office, I was very successful and promoted to area coordinator in Cleveland, Ohio. So, I moved north alone, with plans to bring my family later. That was a big mistake. The new "other woman" was emerging, which was my greed for money. This desire led me lusting for *everything,* because *nothing* was satisfying. I was blind to the fact I was hurting my wife because of the love of money. I didn't realize why setting goals and hitting them was just leading me further into depression.

After a few months in Cleveland, the money started flowing like water over a fall. However, the emptiness was still there and the flowing of money didn't fill the void. One of my friends said, "Tommy would you like to go out and smoke marijuana?" My first response was, "No thanks, I don't drink or do drugs." Then Ed said, "It's all natural. God grew it out of the earth." I reasoned, "Since Ed smokes, and God grew it, it must be okay."

Looking back now, no blame to Ed, it is clear to me that I was succumbing to a temptation that could have killed me. The drugs didn't ease the emptiness. They only numbed me for a few hours in the evening. I started out smoking marijuana one night a week; however, it was not long before I was high all week.

I met Cathy at a Disco Club in Brookpark, which is a suburb of Cleveland. She was a professional dance instructor and wanting to see her more often, led to nightly occurrences in disco clubs. I was going out nightly with my friend Ed and the two other area coordinators smoking dope, drinking, and dancing disco. Ed and I developed a great friendship, and we are still friends 40 years later. Disco music was "the" music back then, and we knew all the disco clubs around Cleveland. One of our disco places was "The Rockside Holiday Inn." One night, I parked my Lincoln in a No Parking Zone, only to come out and find the cops loading it onto a truck. I had a Mafia bumper sticker that said, "MAFIA CAR KEEPA YA HANDSA OFF." I went out ignorantly yelling at the officer, "Can't you see that bumper sticker?" He handcuffed me and I was going to jail for threating an officer. Tony was with me that night, and came out and talked to the officer. I think Tony called the mayor and saved me from going to jail. I was so prideful, full of crap, and myself that I should have gone to jail for a while. That might have saved me from what was coming next.

Going to South Florida and doing the rich man's drug was my new goal. I remember pulling into Pete & Lenny's Supper Club in Ft. Lauderdale, and I fell over my steering wheel and overdosed on cocaine. This was just one of the times that I cheated death. After reading the next chapter, you will wonder how I am still alive.

# 4

# PROTECTED FROM DEATH

After my financial success in Cleveland, the company offered me a position in Ft. Lauderdale, Florida. We immediately packed, and went on our way. There were many people to meet and a lot of money involved. I was looking forward to making thousands of dollars per week and could hardly wait to get the rich man's high: *cocaine*.

The Mafia connections and money increased even more but nothing much had changed from Cleveland. I met Don, who is a realtor, and he assisted us in finding a condominium. We became best friends, and just like Ed from Cleveland, we went out to party just about every night. Just before we moved to Florida, I bought a new Lincoln Town Car: cold black, darkened windows and a glass roof. I worshiped the Mafia. I wanted to dress like the mob, eat Italian food, and drive black cars that looked Mafia. Don't forget the glass roof because it will prove quite significant later in my story.

I always wanted to try the rich man's drug. Smoking weed was awesome, but I wanted to try *cocaine*. I suspected Don was snorting and I was wondering *how long* it would take him to share. Well guess what? One night about 11 p.m., the *long* wait was over. Don and I had been smoking dope and I was starting to crash big time. When you start coming down from a buzz, you just want to go to bed. I wondered why he wasn't tired. I said, "Don I am tired, you had better take me home." Don pulled out a 100 dollar bill and unfolded it. Then he pulled out a straw from his suit pocket. Then he said, "Hawk, take a snort of this, and it will make you feel better." I said, "*Really*?" I hesitated at first, and then we continued with the rich man's high. He fixed up one side of my nose and within about ten seconds, he fixed up the other side. Wow, I could say W O W backwards, forwards and upside down. I felt like I just got up from a good night's sleep, showered, and ready to party all night. The next night I went to meet Don at his friend's house. They were in the back of the house, and when they heard me come in, Don yelled out, "Hawk, the *cocaine* is on the table, help yourself." I observed a straw on the table, and I knew what to do because of the night before. Lying beside the straw was a pile, and two small lines of *cocaine* about the size of matchsticks. I have always been greedy and yes, you know what happened next. Ignorantly, I snorted from the pile. Don came into the room with a look of concern. With a smirk on his face, He asked, "Hawk, what did you do?" I responded, "You told me to help myself!" He just about lost it laughing, along with concern and disbelief. I don't think we returned home until four or five the next morning.

The business continued to grow and I began making more than $1,500 per week. Even though I was making this kind of money, I could hardly pay our rent. We ate our meals off a card table and all three of us were sleeping on the floor on one mattress. Where was the money going? With no thought of my wife and son, I was eating out and partying seven nights a week in the most expensive nightclubs and supper clubs South Florida had to offer. In other words, this hillbilly from Gallia County in Southern Ohio went nuts in Broward County in Southern Florida. My friend Don and I were snorting the best cocaine and smoking the best pot available in South Florida. When you smoke a lot of dope, you constantly need something liquid to refresh your throat and for me that liquid was a Jim Beam and Coke. The depression, that wasn't quenched from the drugs, the alcohol accomplished temporally. Now I had two addictions: *drugs and alcohol.*

One of my favorite places for consuming drinks and disco dancing was Pete and Lenny's in Ft. Lauderdale. I remember one night a police officer followed me into the parking lot and flashed his lights. I was so stoned I could hardly get out of the car, but I had to, because of the dope smell inside. I had to slide along the side of my car to stand up. Finally, I got to the back of my car away from the smell as he approached. I had four pounds of Acapulco gold in the trunk and that was enough to send me to jail for a long time. Somehow, we started talking about country music. He never asked me for my driver license. Did he forget? I don't think so. I believe God was watching out for me because He knew I would be writing this book just for you. How many times has God protected you from death or situations like this one?

A man from the East Coast contacted me about business. In the past, he was always trying to lend me money while I lived in Ohio. After many phone conversations, I wanted to meet him and he wanted to connect with me after I told him how much money I was making.

In all of my involvement with the Mafia, they had failed so far in getting me in their grip. I always rejected any favors; however, unknown to me, this man from the East Coast was setting a trap. A few days later, I picked him up at the Ft. Lauderdale Airport. You talk about a Mafia hardcore look; he looked like one of the stars in the Godfather movie! As he was shutting the door to my car, he said, "Tommy we are going to the race track." Now here was my thinking: "Wow, maybe I can make some money on a race." Little did I know what he had planned as we drove South on I-95 toward Hialeah Park. I didn't realize I was walking blindly into his trap.

After getting out of the car, we walked into the racetrack and there stood a man leaning up against a pole. We walked over to him, and he suggested a horse to bet in the fifth race. I put 500 dollars on the horse to win. I felt like a star in a Mafia movie. In the last few seconds of the race, my horse was so far ahead of the pack; he could have walked in and won. OMG! I was on my way to making thousands of dollars on a horse race. However, in the final seconds, my horse fell and threw his rider and I was let down. However, if my horse had won, the Mafia would have me right where they wanted: *owning* me by *owing* them. When that horse fell, I wondered aloud, "Was that an accident?" Mother was always praying for me and the words of my brother came back: "I love you, you know that don't you?" Does God really love me and is He protecting my family from the grip of the Mafia? Did God send an Angel to trip that horse? I shook it off and continued to idolize my connections.

Just a short time later, I was driving on I-95 South through the city of Ft. Lauderdale. It was dark and I narrowly escaped a rear end collision. The traffic had stopped and all I remember seeing were the bright tail lights. Somehow my car swerved over three lanes of traffic into the curb lane. Once I regained control, I stopped and sat frozen behind the wheel as I felt something I have never felt before: *love*. Thoughts of my brother came again: "I *love* you, you know that don't you?" As I was experiencing this incredible *love*, somehow I experienced what the results would have been if *love* had not shown up.

*"God is Love"* (1st. John 4:8).

Thank God, for a mother who believed in praying! I am sorry, but this is the only way I can explain what happened. I suddenly felt my face sitting on the back of my skull without any pain. From the back of my skull to my face was about three inches. I was stunned and shaken, but thankful that *love* saved my life. Oh, the *love* I was experiencing. (THERE ARE NO WORDS)! I continued with my plans that night and headed to my favorite nightclub. I continued smoking dope and snorting *cocaine* for the next few hours, even though I just had this awesome experience.

I remember sitting at the bar, talking to a woman, and the next thing I remember I was at her house. I had no idea how I got there or where I was. She must have put something in my drink, and now I'm in a freaky-looking place. As I gained a little of my senses, I somehow got out of her house and made it to my car. As I headed out of her driveway, it hit me: "I don't know where I am!" I am not exaggerating this; I didn't know what part of the United States I was in, let alone what town or city. Now you talk about something mind-blowing: the next thing I knew, I was sitting in the driveway of my house. That same voice came again: "I *love* you, you know that don't you?" Then again, I remembered that Bible verse: "*God is Love*." Either an Angel took hold of my car and drove me home or God transported me through a miracle like Enoch.

> "*Enoch walked with God; then he was no more,*
> *because God took him away*" (Genesis 5:24 NIV).

He saved my life earlier that evening; however, I continued to party the rest of the evening. I got into trouble again, and there again was *unconditional love* that never fails. If you think God's love has conditions or you have to keep some rule to get acceptance, a lying spirit deceives you. You need to repent *(change your mind)* in how you see God. He is our Father not our Judge.

The next day, because of my experience with *love* the night before, I remembered the summer time when it was hot and we kids used to go wading in the creeks to keep cool. My friend Monvil and I were wading in Little Bull Skin Creek. I got in water over my head and could not swim. My friend was downstream and didn't hear me yell for help as I was going under. I remember trying to dig my fingers into the bottom and pull myself to the bank. I was ready to give up when a big sandy- haired, tall man put out his hand and pulled me out. When I caught up with Monvil, I told him what had happened and asked, "Who was that man?" Do you remember: The Lone Ranger, "*Who was that masked man*?" Who was that man, Jesus?

Monvil said, "I never saw anyone." I know it was an Angel from the Lord taking care of me again. Oh how He *loves* us! How many *midnights* or times have you cheated death? You know, it is no accident that God put this book in your hands. Write me and let me know, as I would like to share your story: tommyhawk@live.com.

In the bottom of that creek, I was at another *midnight* in my life. As I think about that experience today, many times I ask Jesus, "How many *midnights* have there been that I do not know about?" "How many times has God saved me, knowing, that He was going to use me to write this book just for you?" I am sure you have cheated death many times; you have someone praying for you. Little did I know this love was leading me to: *An offer I couldn't refuse.*

# 5

# AN OFFER I COULDN'T REFUSE

Now I am being set up for an offer I couldn't refuse. The company promoted me from area coordinator to State Director of West Virginia. We left the *beaches* of South Florida for a new beginning in the *mountains* around Charleston.

The Mafia connections and drugs were still the same: plentiful. Actually, I had a drug problem back when I was just a small baby. Every Sunday when the church doors opened, mother D- R- U- G me to church. Ha! The Mafia nightclubs, drugs, and parties looked a lot better than what I had seen in the church. I became a Christian when I was a young boy, and although I ran from religion all those years, thinking I was running from God, He saved my life many times: *His love would not let me go.* The message preached where mother and dad attended church caused me to see God as a judge and a mean child abuser. I figured He was like my dad and just ready to backhand me with a lightning bolt the moment I disobeyed a church rule or sinned.

The continuation of new Mafia connections and more drugs led me deeper into the valley of depression. Believing the lies of Satan always left me unfulfilled and more depressed. However, unknowingly, I always came back for more deception as usual. The company's promotion set me up for the biggest lie of all. Within a few months, my office was number one in sales, and I was making more money than our company president was. The way I looked at it, I had an opportunity to become a multi-millionaire and that would be real living. This time it would be the last of Satan's traps I would fall in. I took his bait of getting rich and ran with it. I had one more god to try: the god of great wealth. I was on my way to making $20,000 to $30,000 a month.

What happened to me at this point reminds me of a story of two men fishing along the Ohio River. The Ohio boy was on one side of the river, while the West Virginia boy was on the other. It was late at night and so foggy they couldn't see each other. The Ohio boy was yelling with great excitement at the fish he was catching. He pulled in another big one and then yelled, "I caught another one." The West Virginia boy had no luck, and heard what was going on across the river. Finally, about midnight he yelled to the Ohio boy in his southern voice,

☻"What are you using to catch all of those fish?"

☺"Worms," he shouted back!

☻The Mountaineer yelled back, "Well, I am using worms and haven't caught a thing!"

☺ "Then why don't you cross the river and fish with me?" the Ohio boy asked.

☻He replied, "I don't have a boat. How do I get over there?"

☺The Buckeye yells back, "I have a strong thirteen-battery flash light and I'll shine it across the foggy river and you just get up and walk on the beam."

☻That hillbilly yells back in his southern voice, "You think I am stupid just because I live in West Virginia? I know what you will do after I get half way across that river, YOU WILL TURN THE LIGHT OUT!"

Satan flashed a deceiving light across to me: a foggy vision to make me believe in a fish- filled river of satisfaction. He used riches as a lure, and the bait was sweet. I swallowed Satan's lie: hook, line, and sinker. The beam of deception deceived me into thinking I would catch a buzz and the results would be fulfillment, just like all the other lies. My thoughts were, "If I can only get to the other side of this wealthy dream and start living with the wealthy of this world, then I will find satisfaction. I will be able to *catch* all the peace and happiness that the rich experience."

I set a goal to make $3,000 per week. You could say my walk to success in Charleston was like walking on that flashlight beam across the Ohio River. I was staying afloat on that beam of deception and soon was earning my goal. That amount would be about $8,000 per week in today's economy.

After getting across the river, I received my first check for $3,000, thus accomplishing my goal. It was like the night of fishing with the man across the river. It was midnight and he hadn't *caught* a fish. Even though I had accomplished my goal, again I felt like a drowning man who had fallen into the chilly water of the Ohio River. That *fish* was not big enough! I set bigger goals to catch bigger fish and just knew more *money* would do the trick. I was on my way to becoming wealthy. However, the bright light of deception was going out and my hopes were fading. As the fish got bigger, any hope of satisfaction became like the Ohio River fog. In this fog of deception, the loneliness and depression was at a new high. I had set many goals and accomplished every one of them except one; through all my efforts, I could not fill the hole, the void inside of me.

I had come to the end of my struggles for acceptance, fulfillment and peace of mind. Yes, I could see my beautiful wife and my awesome son, but only through a dark foggy haze of depression. Nothing was satisfying, including my family or the pleasures of the world, including golf, drugs, and my journey to country music stardom. Now I had caught the largest fish in the river, but like all the rest, it was a dead fish. When you are empty inside, depressed and lonely, nothing sours your stomach like the world's riches. There is no *lasting* satisfaction, only a fleshly (earthly) buzz.

I knew it was either suicide or God. However, instead of attempting suicide, I began searching for Him. I would drive around Charleston in my Mafia-looking Lincoln and my Pin Stripped Suite, weeping and beating my fist on the dash of my car screaming out to Him, "GOD! I know you are real, and I DON'T KNOW HOW I KNOW IT, but I know you are, AND I AM GOING TO FIND YOU."

I often asked myself, "Am I going nuts?"

I do not know how many days or weeks this continued, but one night in June of 1978, I was driving from Columbus to Charleston. I was shouting at the top of my lungs as I continued beating on the dash of my car, "I DON'T KNOW HOW I KNOW IT, but I know you are real. I AM GOING TO FIND YOU IF IT IS THE LAST THING I DO!"

The money did not soothe my misery and this reminds me of a true story Billy Graham shared in his book, THE KEY TO PERSONAL PEACE.

He wrote, *"My wife, Ruth, and I once visited an Island in the Caribbean. One of the wealthiest men in the world asked us to come to his lavish home for lunch. He was seventy-four years old and throughout the entire meal, he seemed close to tears. He said, "I am the most miserable man in the world. Out there is my yacht, private plane and helicopters; yet I am miserable."*

That little story described my *lost,* miserable life. I have heard so many people say, "I found the Lord." He was never *lost*; I was the one who was lost in the icy freezing water of this world's 666 system (*man, man, man*). I was trying to find something to fill the hole inside of me; however, no *man* or woman had the answer. I had come to the end of trying. Little did I know that I would be getting *an offer I couldn't refuse.*

As I continued down the highway on Route 35 toward Gallipolis, I was just west of Rio Grande. I was slamming my fist on the dash of my car, shouting at God again from down in the depths of my heart. Only this time I began to weep and tears were gushing out of my eyes, flooding down my cheeks and dripping off my chin. My pin striped suit coat and tie was soaked. I could not see the road clearly. As this amazing love flooded me, I pulled over to side of the road by a little town called Centerville. Even now over 30 years later, I have no sufficient words of explanation. Do you remember me writing earlier about the glass roof in my new Lincoln? I immediately looked up through that glass roof, through a flood of water; I saw the most beautiful flower. The flower was pink and appeared as a cross between a rose and a tulip. I was still weeping as this washing and cleansing continued inside.

"*He might sanctify her, having cleansed her by the washing of water with the word*" (Ephesians. 5:26 NAS).

The evidence of emotional healing was flowing through my eyes. Love was washing and healing my wounds:

*"He Himself bore our sins in His body on the Cross, so that we might die to sin and live to righteousness; for by His wounds you were healed"* (1st. Peter 2:24, emphasis mine).

Again looking through the flood of tears into heaven, I saw gold. Out of my mouth came these words. "Wow, gold you can see through?"

*"The twelve gates were made of pearls--each gate from a single pearl! And the main street was pure gold, as clear as glass"* (Revelation 21:21 NLT, emphasis mine).

I am so sorry, but this next part of my story is so hard to put into words. This experience was like surgery as someone was opening my chest and sticking a spout of love down in that empty hole. As I bent my body over my steering wheel, I was weeping, sobbing because of these waves of liquid love. It seemed like it was liquid. *How could I refuse this love*? It felt like there was a river of water flowing out of my eyes. As I am writing this, the tears are flowing again. Oh, it is even harder to put what happened next into words.

*There were waves of liquid love flowing into that spout, flooding that hole and it was flowing to every part of me. As a result, out came a flood of liquid flowing down my face.*

Oh, I pray that you are feeling this love-anointing right now. If you want this kind of love, just close your eyes and as an act of faith say, *"Jesus, I receive this love."* Again, I remembered those words from my brother, "I love you, you know that don't you?" That is what God is saying to you right now, as you continue reading. As this experience continued, I wanted to let this love flow out of me. I was so full of love I would have kissed a fence post. I was so full of this river of love, I wanted to stop someone on the highway and just let it flow out of me to everyone.

*"He who believes in Me as the Scripture said 'From his innermost being will flow rivers of living water'"* (John 7:38 NASB).

This living water (love) was flowing into me by His Holy Spirit through waves of liquid love and I wanted to let it flow to someone else. I really had no idea that the great preacher Charles Finney had a similar experience. He wrote the following about it:

*I began to weep. It seemed as if my heart was all-liquid; and my feelings were in such a state that I could not hear my own voice in singing without causing my sensibility to overflow. I wondered at this, and tried to suppress my tears, but could not. After trying in vain to suppress my tears, I put up my instrument and stopped singing. There was no fire, and no light, in the room; nevertheless, it appeared to me as if it were perfectly lighted. As I went in and shut the door after me, it seemed as if I met the Lord Jesus Christ face to face. It did not occur to me then, nor did it for some time afterward, that it was wholly a mental state. On the contrary, it seemed to me that I saw him as I would see any other man. He said nothing, but looked at me in such a manner as to break me right down at his feet. I have always since regarded this as is most remarkable state of mind; for it seemed to me a reality, that he stood before me, and I fell down at his feet and poured out my soul to him. I wept aloud like a child, and made such confessions as I could with my choked utterance. It seemed to me that I bathed his feet with my tears; and yet I had no distinct impression that I touched him, that I recollect. I must have continued in this state for a good while; but my mind was too much absorbed with the interview to recollect anything that I said. But I know, as soon as my mind became calm enough to break off from the interview, I returned to the front office, and found that the fire that I had made of large wood was nearly burned out. But as I turned and was about to take a seat by the fire, I received the mighty baptism of the Holy Ghost. Without any expectation of it, without ever having the thought in my mind that there was any such thing for me, without any recollection that I had ever heard the thing mentioned by any person in the world, the Holy Spirit descended upon me in a manner that seemed to go through me, body and soul. I could feel the impression, like a wave of electricity, going through and through me. Indeed, it seemed to come in waves and waves of liquid love; for I could not express it in any other way. It seemed like the very breath of God. I can recollect distinctly that it seemed to fan me, like immense wings. No words can express the wonderful love that was shed abroad in my heart. I wept aloud with joy and love; and I do not know but I should say, I literally bellowed out unutterable gushing's of my heart. These waves came over me, and over me, and over me, one after the other, until I recollect I cried out, "I shall die if these waves continue to pass over me." I said, "Lord, I cannot bear any more;" yet I had no fear of death.*

*In this state, I was taught the doctrine of justification by faith, as a present experience. That doctrine had never taken any such possession of my mind, that I had ever viewed it distinctly as a fundamental doctrine of the Gospel. Indeed, I did not know at all what it meant in the proper sense. But I could now see and understand what was meant by the passage, "Being justified by faith, we have peace with God through our Lord Jesus Christ." I could see that the moment I believed, while up in the woods, all sense of condemnation had entirely dropped out of my mind; and that from that moment I could not feel a sense of guilt or condemnation by any effort that I could make. My sense of guilt was gone; my sins were gone; and I do not think I felt any more sense of guilt than if I never had sinned. This was just the revelation that I needed. I felt myself justified by faith; and so far as I could see, I was in a state in which I did not sin. Instead of feeling that I was sinning all the time, my heart was so full of love that it overflowed. My cup ran over with blessing and with love; and I could not feel that I was sinning against God. Nor could I recover the least sense of guilt for my past or future sins. Of this experience I said nothing that I recollect, at the time, to anybody; that is, of this experience of justification.*

Source: Charles Finney - Grandson,
*Memoirs of Reverend Charles G. Finney*
New York: A.S. Barnes, 1876), 13–23.

I have asked Jesus many times over the years, "Why did you come to me personally in 1978 pouring your love into me?"

It is May 10, 2013, I was sitting at a Panera Bread Store in Reynoldsburg, Ohio, editing this book, and I asked Him again. This time He spoke and here is what He said,

"I wanted people to read what you would be writing.

There are multitudes of hurting people who need to experience My healing Love.

I want them to enjoy living, and to be free from the fears of this world's 666 system and rest in My Kingdom. There is no rest in the world's system; that is why so many are fearful.

I want them to experience the same love that I gave you.

I want them to know through your writings that I love them and that they are special.

My love burns for those who really do not know Me and for many in My Body who are caught up in trying to find satisfaction in the world's system. If they will just put away their pre-conceived ideas about Me and get to know me as their Father and Friend. They don't have to perform to experience My Love, just receive it by faith."

Like Mr. Finney, that night at the foot of that Cross, I experienced what I was fishing for in this world's system for years. Finally, I have found what I was looking for. I have also found in my walk with Jesus: as soon as you win a battle in one area, Satan comes again in a different way to take you captive.

There was another trap set for me: taking me captive through Christian legalistic religion. There is a difference between Christian legalistic religion and the Christian life. Anti-Christ Christian religion based on rules and regulations, produces **D**eath (death with a capitol **D**, no *lasting* peace of mind or joy). Same results as living in the worlds system. Adding rules, regulations or the Ten Commandments to the Cross makes it anti-Christ and Cross gospel giving the same results (**D**eath No life). The Christian life is Jesus plus nothing.

Christian life is the life of Jesus' (*Love*) flowing *in* you, *through* you, and *as* you by His Holy Spirit.

Like Mr. Finney, this was the first time in my Christian life that I felt love. Everything I pursued in fulfilling my emptiness, I found that night. What I looked for in organized religion, drugs, parties, cocaine, dope, new cars, golf, flying in a Learjet, and all the other lusts (strong desires), I found that night when Jesus made Himself real to me by His love. If you are fellowshipping in the right church, there is an anointing of unconditional love flowing from the minister. You are reading this book and maybe you are unsaved or maybe you are a Christian. My question is this, are you hurting and do you relate to some of my story? Please, think about these few words.

I smoked the best dope and snorted the best cocaine the Mafia had to offer.

I partied in the most expensive nightclubs that South Florida and Cleveland, Ohio, had to offer. There was no life, (lasting satisfaction) in the pleasures that this world's system had to offer. I hope it don't take you as long to find this out as it did me.

I was in **D**ead Christian religion for years and continued to ask the question, "Where is the beef?" I was tired of trying to keep the Ten Commandments and church rules. The more I tried to obey the law and church rules, the more I sinned.

*"I do not frustrate the grace of God: for if righteousness come by the law, then Christ is dead in vain"* (Galatians 2:21).

Christian religion is more deceiving than what I experienced in Mafia connections. If your church is trying to put you under the law, tell them you are not an Old Testament Jew, but a Gentile and *refuse their offer.*

Now back to my experience and here is my point: There is nothing in the world's system (666: man, man, man) and Christian religion that gives lasting peace. I hate to say this, but much of Christian religion is worse than the world's system. Many Christians believe that if you are having fun, you are not being spiritual, and should feel guilty. Example: In the past, if I was on the golf course, I always felt guilty. Satan's lie was, "you should be at home praying and reading your Bible." I would carry a little green new testament with me on the cart, and while riding down the fairway, I would read, trying to soothe my guilt and missing fellowshipping with my Christian Brother. I didn't know about this scripture,

*"There is no condemnation [or guilt] to those who are in Christ Jesus"* (Romans 8:1, emphasis mine).

When you are under the law or denominational rules, it is hard to have fun. At least in the world's system you can have some fun, but not in extreme Christian religion. There is always something religious you should be doing to please God. Religion hinders the life of Jesus flowing out of you. Here is the answer:

God loves you and wants you to accept His awesome love through the Lord Jesus Christ, who is alive and wants you to know Him. We all get tricked by Satan into trying to fulfill ourselves with the world's pleasures. Because of guilt and condemnation, many times we go back under the Law of Moses, church rules, or the traditions of our denominations and try to find fulfillment. There is only one thing that satisfies God's creation: The love of Jesus.

I remember speaking at Trinity United Methodist Church in Pickerington, OH, and prior to pastor Scott Kelso introducing me, he made this statement: "The world's system has nothing that can ever truly *fulfill* a Christian."

I would like to add to his statement. The world's 666 system and

Christian religion (the preaching of the Jewish Law or church rules), can never *truly fulfill* a child of God or the unsaved. The life of God is Jesus IN you, THROUGH you, and AS you, the hope of Glory. It is not you trying to be like Jesus, it is you going on an *eternal vacation* from your own *works* by letting Him be Himself through you: His yoke is easy. The next question for me was, "How do I do that?" This answer is so simple, but challenging because Satan will try to stop you through fear, as he did me.

Find a church that line up with the statements below.

☺ All teaching is saturated with the message of grace (unconditional love).

☻ No teaching of the Old Covenant law given to the Jews; we are gentiles.

☺ All of their messages are centered on the finished work of the Cross.

☻ No church rules, traditions of men or of a denomination.

☺ All of the messages have Jesus as the core of the teaching.

☻ No teaching of The Ten Commandments.

To sum up the above statements, if you go to a church and hear messages that put you under guilt and condemnation, run to another church. Believe me, I understand the fear that Satan brings by your Christian friends. My mentor, Malcolm Smith, said, "Whatever you believe, is it working? If it is not, then there is something that you believe is error or false teaching."

After my encounter with Jesus and the many years of thinking about God's unconditional love, all I want to do is tell you how much He loves you. The major reason I have written this book, was to pass on these words from Jesus that came through Freddie's lips, "I love you, you know that don't you?" I know now it was Jesus speaking those words through my brother.

After this great encounter with Jesus, I still could not kick the bondage of drugs. I would flush drugs down the commode and the next day I was on a flight back to Florida to buy more.

"Do you mean to tell me, Tommy that if you had died while hooked on drugs that you would have went to be with Jesus?" That is like asking me, "Tommy, do you mean to tell me that when you were 65 lbs. over- weight and Jesus came back right after you had stuffed yourself with food and died from a heart attack, that you would have still go to heaven?" ABSOLUTELY.

YES! I know Christian religion hates what I just wrote. His Law will condemn us but His Grace *saves* us, and His Grace *sustains* us. It is Jesus plus nothing. If we stay saved by good works (obeying church rules etc.), we could boast: "Look at me I have kept the rules and traditions of our church."

*"For it is by grace you have been saved, through faith--and this is* ***not*** *from yourselves, it is the gift of God"* (Ephesians 2:8 NIV, bold emphasis added).

My encounter with Jesus set me free in my spirit, but I was not experiencing total freedom in my soul (mind, will, and emotions). You may have become a Christian earlier in life but because of well-meaning Christians, pastors, Bible teachers and legalistic teachings, maybe you thought Jesus had left you. Well, that is a religious lie, a God in their making. You may have sinned, but His Word says:

*"For I will be merciful to their unrighteousness and I will remember their sins*

*no more" (Hebrews 8:12 NEHB).*

However, like me, maybe you have believed the lies from Christian religion that taught you to perform to stay saved. I was teaching at a Bible college a few years ago on the subject of God's unconditional love. I made this statement: "If I would have died while I was still in bondage to drugs, I would have gone to heaven." The snake of Christian religion hissed, and that was the last time I was invited. This drug bondage went on for weeks until one evening I was sitting at a traffic light beside the Charleston West Virginia Police Station. I was talking to God about the drugs and about my inability to stop. I said to Him, "Jesus, I do not want to be controlled by these drugs, but now I know that I can't stop in my own effort." Therefore, with a tongue in cheek smile and an attitude of challenging Him, I said, "Lord if you don't take these drugs away from me while I am still alive, when I die, I will come to heaven buzzed." I just know He laughed. He just wanted me to know that through Him I can do all things. I didn't defeat drugs through my own effort (or law-rule), but when I gave my problem to Him. I was open and honest with my feelings and emotions. The battle of my effort to stop was over. This is what you call "casting your cares upon Him" (1 Peter 5:7).

*"I can do all things through Christ who strengthens me"* (Philippians 4:13 KJV).

After that little conversation with Him, I noticed a desire to study my Bible. I read for an hour or so and then I would do some drugs. When I share this, people will say, "You have to be kidding me, Tommy. Are you saying you would read God's word and then get high?" "No, I didn't say I got high; I smoked some dope." I was experiencing such a buzz on God's Word; the drugs were destroying the beautiful experience of love I was feeling from my Father. As I continued studying God's word, I felt like a hypocrite because of what Christian religion had taught me. Here is an example of their religious questions: "What if Jesus came back and you were smoking dope or in one of those old hell-holes (bar rooms) doing karaoke?"

Most people love it when I sing karaoke songs like, "A Long Black Train" or "The Night Old Jack Daniels met John 3:16." The anointing of love flows to everyone in the restaurant. The results are: Jesus is glorified, lifted up, and many come with questions about the song and John 3:16.

*"For God loved the world (you and I) so much that he gave his one and only Son, so that everyone who believes in Him will not perish but <u>have</u> (not get) eternal life"* (John 3:16, emphasis added).

Do you think it would be OK if Jesus came back and I was singing karaoke? I remember a person asking this question. "Do you really think you should be in a place where they sell liquor? What if Jesus came back while you were in there?" I replied, "Well He might have a glass of wine with me before He took me with Him. You know He was good at wine making?" His facial expression dropped as he changed the subject.

As I continued in God's Word, the temptation for drugs slowly disappeared. Nothing had changed from Florida concerning my fleshly desires but I was still trying to fill the emptiness by going to the Charleston Night Clubs seven nights a week. Something was happening: as my desire to read my Bible *increased,* my desire to go out at night and do drugs *decreased.*

Little did I know my wife was planning on taking our son and leaving. Here is what was happening: As I would study God's word, it put me on a *spiritual high* or as they say on the streets, "I got buzzed." The buzz I was getting from His Word was better than what I was getting from the drugs, alcohol, and wild parties. I was in the process of deliverance from the *counterfeit high* while experiencing the real thing from God's Word. Now I was beginning to see the buzz from the world's system for what it was: a *counterfeit.*

In light of what I just shared, years later, I was speaking at a prison in Oregon. I was telling the men how God was *blessing* me, and how it was so much better than the drugs. The men really didn't know what I meant by God's *blessing*, so I changed it to *buzzing* me and then they shouted out, "God *buzz* you Tommy." As I was leaving, many of the inmates came up to me and shook my hand and said, "God buzz you Tommy." I have spoken in many prisons and I always ask this question before I closed the meeting. "How many of you men had a good relationship with your dad?" I have yet to see one hand go up. I want to say this to all you prisoners: "You have a heavenly Father who loves you. No matter what you have done, you are the apple of His eye. He made you special and I can prove it. Look at one of your fingerprints. No one has or ever will have your print. God made you special." I am hoping I get invited to speak where ever you are.

After a few weeks of being buzzed on God's Word, the going-out nights was one or two nights a week. I was just sitting home buzzed by reading my Bible. Within a few weeks, I stopped going out. My wife saw all of this happening and she told me later she thought I found out about her getting ready to leave. God's Word became alive to me, and I spent several hours daily just meditating and studying. Like Mr. Finney, in those rich fulfilling moments, I realized that Jesus had paid the price for my past, present, and future sins. The evidence was His unconditional liquid love we both experienced.

Many years ago, as a young boy, I accepted His Word (Jesus) and chose to believe there is only one payment for sin, and that was His blood.

"*For Christ died for sins once and for all*" (1 Peter 3:18, NIV).

That means for all people and all your sins, past, present and future (but not the *Godfather* way). As they would say in the Mafia,

"We have contacts with judges and we got your rap sheet cleared." In the Kingdom of God, Jesus does not have a rap sheet with your name on it because His word says:

*"God is love"* (1 John 4:8).
*"Love keeps no record of wrongs"* (1 Cor. 13:5, NAS).

You have no rap sheet because He prophetically said:

*I, even I, am the One who wipes out your transgressions for My own sake, And I will* **not** *remember your sins"* (Isaiah.43:25, emphasis mine).

Then the writer of Hebrews reminds us of what God said through Isaiah:

*"I will forgive their wickedness, and I will never again remember their sins"* (Hebrews 8:12 NLT, emphasis mine).

Jesus is our contact and through His blood, He cleared our record by hanging our rap sheet on the Cross: He became our sin. Because of *God our Father* sacrificing His Son through the shedding of His blood, we are free. Many preachers will cause you to remember your sins, but not God.

I have a purpose for living now. In the past, I just lived, captured by the lust (strong desire) of my flesh. I finally realized that it was producing **D**eath in me (with a Capitol **D**): **no life**. I am now His and have His very life inside me. The world's system has the mark of the beast (ways of the world) in their forehead (their brain) but in God's Word, it says:

*Then I looked, and behold, the Lamb was standing on Mount Zion, and with Him one hundred and forty-four thousand* [**symbolic of the church**], *having His name and the name of His Father written on their foreheads"*

(Revelation 14:1).

God has marked our foreheads, and that gives us peace of mind because He says by this mark, "You are Mine." It is like this: Everything Satan has in this world's system (dope, cocaine, alcohol etc.) only numbs the pain, which is just a *counterfeit for the buzz* you get from His Holy Spirit. Jesus came not to cover our emotional pain, but bring healing *in* our emotions.

*"By His wounds we are healed"* (1st. Peter 2:24).

Satan's counterfeit is to numb us by this world's system, including his destructive distractions like *Hollywood*. However, *Hollywood* is no match for the reality of God's *HolyWord* living in us. When *Hollywood actors* become more important than His *HolyWord Apostles*, Satan has trapped you into believing the lie that an hour or two of *Hollywood* can bring you peace of mind. Whatever is at the center of your daily conversations is what you are feeding on.

"I can live independently of God" was *the* lie in the Garden of Eden. Every generation since then has continued to believe *the* lie. We believe the same lie today; I can find fulfillment through movies, rather than trusting Him and the moving of His Holy Spirit. The deception is, somehow *Hollywood* will produce peace of mind. Only the Prince of Peace, Jesus, can heal your emotions and give you real peace. *Hollywood* only covers or numbs the pain for a couple of hours by keeping your mind off your hunger to know Jesus.

His love was like the hound of heaven, always on my trail. Even though I thought I was running from God, in reality, I was not running from God but from mean, legalistic religion. Religion told me the lie that I was running from God. When I say religion, I am talking about corporate legalistic rules from denominational headquarters. A headquarters-type Godfather "witchcraft spirit" will *whack* you with guilt and condemnation if you do not obey their rules and regulations. How can you run from Jesus who is love, who accepts you and will never reject or leave you? Love always wins.

*"Keep your life free from love of money, and be content with what you have, for he has said, 'I will never leave you nor forsake you"* (Hebrews 13:5, ESV).

I traveled for many years telling my story of freedom from the grip of the Mafia, including interviews with newspapers, television talk shows, and global publications. One was *Voice Magazine*, which is part of The Full Gospel Business Men's Fellowship International. I still receive letters from all across the world from people who have read my story. Many other letters came from television appearances on Trinity Broadcast Network (TBN), Christian Broadcast Network (CBN), Pat Robertson's 700 Club, and many churches in many parts of the world. I traveled for years telling my story of deliverance from the mob. I had concluded that it all started over a misunderstanding concerning a hotel bill while in Cleveland.

While there negotiating a 10 million dollar loan for our company, I was staying at a Swingos Celebrity Hotel downtown. When I checked out, I was 20 dollars short in paying my bill. I promised to send the hotel a check when I returned to Charleston. My assumption was that the mob got the wrong information and didn't pay my bill. As strange as this may sound, they never contacted me again, and for over twenty years I thought it was the hotel bill. However, this just didn't make any sense. I couldn't figure out why they never called again. Would they let 20 dollars stop them from making millions? I spoke on a global scale and shared how I was set free from the mob over a 20-dollar hotel bill in Cleveland. Every time I gave my story, I just could not make sense out of it. Why didn't they call me back to get this problem straightened out?

On April 30, while writing this book, God spoke to me and told me that He used Tony to spring the trap of Satan. It was not the $20 hotel bill, which caused the deal to go bad, it was God showing love to me again, this time through Tony. As Paul Harvey would say, "Now you know the rest of the story." Now it all made sense to me, and was believable, because when I was talking to *the people* in Cleveland, Tony just sat there with that sick concerned look on his face expressing, "You don't know what you are getting into." Even to this day, I really don't know what Tony did that stopped them. I will never forget him and how God used him to free me from what would have been today a $30 Million loan. Tony was such a lover of people. He was such a moral, generous, and caring Italian man. I was speaking in Cleveland many years later at a Full Gospel Business Men's Convention and Tony came to hear me. However, since I do not give altar calls in meetings, because an altar was a place of **death** in the Old Testament, I gave a "Cross" call, which is a place for people to receive the **Life of** Jesus.

Religious altar calls are a time in the meeting where Christians go to make more commitments. They re-dedicate and make new dedications to try again and harder to live the Christian life. Granted, some unsaved will receive Christ as Lord and Savior at an altar call.

A Cross call is not for Christians but the unsaved to receive the gift of salvation. I do give Cross calls for Christians, but this is a ministry call for Christians who are hurting and need prayer. They come forward for ministry but there are no dedications or re-dedications in this call, just a time for them to receive the love of Jesus. This time I gave a Cross call and Tony stood and received the Gospel of the Cross-, and it floored me. Tony was almost deaf and God restored his hearing that night. I wondered if that was God's little way of saying "thank you" to Tony.

As I travel and speak to businesspersons, conventions, prisoners, churches, and Christian events, about the message of God's unconditional love, many choose to believe that the gospel is true after hearing or reading my story. They begin to understand that no matter what they have done or are doing, they do not have to meet any conditions for God's unconditional love. Repentance means: simply changing your mind about what you have believed. Love always wins, and when you come to Him as you are with total trust that He loves you, "*He will begin to* live His life *in* you, *through* you and *as* you." It is so awesome that, according to the scripture below, it is not even your faith.

"*I have been crucified with Christ; it is no longer I who live, but Christ lives in me; and the life which I now live in the flesh (body) I live by* ***the faith of*** *the Son of God, who loved me and gave Himself for me*" (Galatians 2:20 KJV, emphases mine).

His life is your new life. The blue of the sky will look so pure, you will hear the birds sing again, the autumn season will be more beautiful and the snow whiter. You will hear the words, "I love you, you know that don't you?"

# 6

# MAFIA BUZZWORDS

*Warning:* Whatever Christian religion believes, they will not let the facts of scripture upset their traditional beliefs. You are going to read some words that will go against many of the teachings passed down from generations. Some are literally leading gullible church people into a religious Mafia type cultish atmosphere. Example: You must try your best not to sin, yet the scripture says, "He remembers our sin NO more." If you are religious or trying your best not to sin by keeping the rules, this above scripture above could easily anger you.

Because of phrases full of Christian buzzwords like, "You have to try your best," "you have to do your part," "after all, He has done for you, the least you can do is," "You have to stay in fellowship with Him," and the list goes on, with things like trying to keep the Ten Commandments. Grace takes you from "have to" to "get too" so I encourage you to read this carefully and prayerfully. If you are hurting, depressed, and struggling to find peace in your Christian life, I know this chapter will give you hope.

MAFIA BUZZ WORDS
*WHACK*: To have someone killed.

*Good news*: God is not out to *whack* you! Every word in this chapter is meant to encourage and give you hope of enjoying the life God.

I am sure you can relate to my "death" story and to some of the disappointments. I could have said my "life" story but there really was no life (lasting joy and peace of mind) until I was 36 years old.

Do you remember the cross at Rio Grande, Ohio? I was realizing that beautiful spring night that the scripture says:

"*It is no longer I who live, but Christ lives in me. So I live in this earthly body by the faith of the Son of God, who loved me and gave himself for me*" (Galatians 2:20 KJV, emphasis mine).

Notice that it is not our faith but His. At that time, Jesus began to live His Life *in* me, *through* me and *as* me. At that cross, it was Jesus manifesting Himself in me by His Holy Spirit with the only real evidence: Unconditional love.

I was only about 10 years old the night I believed Jesus paid the penalty for all my sins. I will never forget the wonderful feeling of love, joy, and peace the night I accepted His sacrifice for me. No words can accurately render what I felt. I remember telling mother, "If had known that it felt this good, I would have done it years ago." When I came home that night from Big Four Church, a little old country church, and I felt so wonderful. Jesus accepted me just as the song that Billy Graham used, "Just as I am without one plea." I didn't have to beg or make promises to Him. That week was so wonderful, peaceful, and fulfilling. Jesus was living His life *in* me, *through* me, and *as* me. Little did I know that Satan had put a religious contract out to *whack* me because I choose to believe in Jesus.

The next Sunday, Satan was hiding in shadows of the "religious mob." Everyone had religious machine guns loaded with religious church laws. They mobbed me, shooting me full of fear holes. They loaded me up with plea after plea and promise after promise. Over the months and years, they told me: If I didn't comply, He would turn His back to me and I would be out of fellowship with God. I would backslide and lose my salvation.

Here are three of the promises I had to make.

1. I must do my best to keep the Ten Commandments and church rules.
2. I must never miss church.
3. I must read my Bible every day or I would fall from grace.

Law *demands* while grace *teaches*. My beautiful experience with Jesus was overshadowed by fear that God would be mad at me if I didn't at least try to keep all the plea's and church rules. Then here comes the religious guilt statement. "After all God has done for you, the least you can do is your best trying to live for God."

I hear so many people at Karaoke say, "They have backslid and are away from God." As you think about that last statement, let me give you something to ponder. Try finding a place in the New Testament that mentions backsliding. It is only in one part of the Old Testament. The Prophet Jeremiah, known as the weeping prophet because much of his writings dealt with the prophetic judgment of

God, never spoke to an individual; only to a nation. This was to the whole nation of Israel because of their backsliding and idolatry.

In contrast, read these New Covenant promises:

*"I will never leave or forsake you"* (Hebrews 13:5).

*"I will forgive their wickedness, and I will never again remember their sins"* (Hebrew 8:12).

Now it would take a religious person to help you to misunderstand that. Now did Jesus lie when He said those words through the writer of Hebrews? In the old covenant, God did remember their sins and lawless deeds. Once a year they shed the blood of animals for a covering, ***not*** a cleansing. When Jesus shed His Blood, it was for cleansing. Under the New Covenant, He does not remember our sins. It is a *"once for all sins"* salvation. "It is finished."

The next Sunday, I was given more warning about rules and promises to keep from backsliding. We had rules that the Jews in the old covenant would have never thought of. Now let me say this, the people who were trying to help me were Christians who themselves were being controlled by fear unknowingly. Their motives were good; they were trying to keeping me from backsliding: their theology was wrong. Again, unknowingly, this is their way to use *fences* to control the congregation: thinking they are keeping us saved.

## FENCES

A fence is a rule that a denomination will construct to keep you from breaking one of the Ten Commandments or church rules. I will explain more about fences later in this chapter. My earlier teachers were *sincere* but now I know they were *sincerely* wrong. I was never taught that I had received eternal life but that it could be a temporary life. If I didn't stay inside the *fences* or color inside the denominational lines and endure until the end of my life I would split hell wide open. What encouragement for a new Christian!

Then there are the extreme Religious Mobs. They will *whack* you by forming a click against you and spurn your name as a heretic if you believe that there are no conditions in experiencing God's love. They teach you to keep their church traditions and see God as a judge rather than a loving father. Jesus talked about them:

*"And so you cancel the word of God in order to hand down your own tradition"* (Mark 7:13).

Example: They will tell you that you have fallen from grace and lost your salvation, if you don't keep the rules, thus staying religiously correct. If a woman comes into an ultra-religious church wearing makeup or pants, some churches will get out their Bible machine guns, *whack* her with bullets of fear, and escort her out.

As the years went by, I was taught that the thief in John 10:10 was Satan. But there is no evidence that Satan is the thief. Is he in the background as a tool? Absolutely! He is secretly using the old covenant law, church rules, and today's religious regulations and traditions to take God's people captive. Satan used the Mafia of Christian religion to steal, *whack*, and destroy my peace and joy for twenty years.

I know that the thief is using ministers today, as he did me, unknowingly in many churches to preach Old Covenant law by trying to marry Jesus to Moses. They use fear of breaking church rules and regulations for higher attendance and financial gain. I know in many cases, it is unknowingly because the man who is writing this book was one of them. Have we let our ministers make God our Father into a type of Godfather, using the law and *fences* of "thou shall not" or "thou must" to control us through fear? On the cross Jesus said, "It is finished." Didn't Jesus do all the *doing?* Now we just do all the believing and *receiving*.

One of the *fences* to keep us from going to hell was tithing. I personally heard a minister in a Word of Faith Church say, "If you don't tithe, you are going to Hell!" Sorry that is NOT a Word of Faith. That is a word of works motivated by fear and greed, producing a works mentality to stay saved. So it must be Jesus plus tithing that keeps us saved? I had a man ask me the other day if I believed in tithing. I said, "Yes, if you are an Old Covenant Jew. We are Gentiles and Gentiles were never given the law."

**BUZZWORD 2**

(Mafia Made Guy)

He is an indoctrinated member of the Mafia family.

Religiously Correct Made Guy:

For years this person is indoctrinated with a mixture of the Gospel of Grace to be saved and then put under the law or church rules to stay saved. They are teaching the traditions of men rather than the Gospel that Paul preached.

When it comes to being a "religiously correct made Christian," I was a made guy for many years. However, I remind you, like others, I didn't know it. I would say, in my opinion, that many ministers today are doing the same thing unknowingly because they too were taught to be correct in their religious beliefs and performance. Many ministers have seen the light of God's Grace, but they know that preaching unconditional love and loosening up on the teachings of their denomination could get them *whacked*. They could lose their retirement savings and would have to start a new church. Let me say this: "I would rather lose a congregation of thousands and start with one person rather than be in bondage to Christian legalistic religion.

Here's a comparison of how the Mafia and Christian Religion works:

• The Mafia Godfather makes you offers and if you refuse, he promises you death.

• The Godfathers of Christian religion makes offers that if you refuse, you'll get worse than death. You spend the rest of your life trying rather than trusting Jesus to live His life through you. I know because I lived in a *religiously correct* performance for years. Because of bondage to rules and religious expectations, peace and joy had no part of me.

God our Father makes us *an offer that is impossible to refuse*. "Ok, Tommy why do so many reject the gospel?" They are not rejecting the gospel. They, like I once did, are rejecting religion. I personally didn't reject Jesus. I was rebelling and rejecting mean religious people. All I ever heard was, "*You are going to hell!*" I don't remember anyone ever saying, "I love you Tommy or that Jesus loved me." The only time I ever heard that someone loved me were those words I have been hearing for years now. Repeatedly in my mind the words from my brother: *"I love you, you know that don't you?"* It is impossible to reject the true gospel. The world is just sick of religious people telling them if they don't repent, they are going burn in hell rather than the church loving them into heaven. A mean condemning judgmental attitude will always fail, but love never does.

Here is an example of my indoctrination causing me to be religiously correct: "God is watching you, so you had better walk that straight and narrow path and not sin." In other words, you better stay within the denominational *fences* of: "*thou shall not and thou shall.*" I remember a little *fence* song my sister Bonnie used to sing in church when she was a little girl. She would point with her little index finger first to her eyes and then to her ears; and sing these lyrics.

"Little eyes, be careful what you see, little ears be careful what you hear, for the savior is up above and He is looking down below, so be careful what you do." Do you see the fear that is attached to that little song? How are we to be careful what we see and hear? I hear pastors every week say, "You better be careful with that message of grace." In other words; I better be careful with trusting that Jesus has done it all. They don't realize that if they are not preaching grace they are Not preaching Jesus. They are preaching an anti-Christ gospel because Jesus is the Grace of God. When you really know Jesus, you will believe the scripture that says:

"*I will never leave or forsake you*" (Hebrews 13:5).

"If we buy the lie that God sits in a swivel chair, ready to rotate His face away when we sin, then we proclaim a God of conditional love and conditional fellowship. But this is to ignore the work of Jesus, who on the cross cried out, "My God, my God, why have you forsaken me?" (Matthew 27:46). Jesus was out of fellowship with his Father so we would never be. (Andrew Farley, *The Naked Gospel* Page 157).

Pastor Farley also said in one of his teachings, when I was good, (not sinning, keeping the law or church rules, tithing etc.) He was always smiling. However, if I messed up, He would swivel around and turn His back to me. Then when I went to the altar and begged

Him to forgive me, He would swivel back around with a smile of acceptance"

Have you ever sat under a minister and his focus was NOT Jesus but sin? Satan has caused many to look over this scripture hundreds of times.

"*Sin is no longer your master, for you no longer live under the requirements of the law. Instead, you live under the freedom of God's grace*" (Romans 6:16).

More examples of the Christian Religion type Mafia includes rules like: only gospel music, Christian Television, G-rated movies or only Christian movies are acceptable. Most of the gospel music and Christian Television is toxic with political correctness. In other words, the Boss-Don-Godfather is warning you from His swivel chair at headquarters and eventually He will hear that you are not coloring within the lines. If you are a pastor and God gives you a revelation that doesn't agree with the headquarters creed, and you preach it, the boss will send a territorial hit-man. He will have his biblical machine gun and "*whack*" you with bullets of condemnation and threats of being fired if you don't preach the denomination's traditional laws (rules). Your future with that religiously correct organization can cause you to walk by fear rather than by faith.

The Jews had the Ten Commandments and were so dedicated to keeping them that they would build *fences* to keep from breaking them but still could not. They had six hundred and thirteen laws and continued to add rules (fences) to help them obey.

Here are a couple of *fences* the Jews constructed to keep from breaking the Sabbath:

*Fence 1:* You shall not drag a chair across the room because of the dust on the floor. Separating the dust, that would be plowing thus breaking the commandment of: *"You shall not work on the Sabbath"* (Exodus 20:10).

*Fence 2*: Women cannot look in the mirror on the Sabbath because if they saw a hair on their chin, they would be tempted to pluck it out and that would be working.

These were a couple of the *fences* erected to keep from breaking the Sabbath. In my opinion, many of the churches who are trying to keep the Ten Commandments are just as bad about erecting *fences.* Many Christians are worse than the Old Covenant Jews. Here is what is so sad; we are Gentiles and never given the Jewish Law.

Here are a few of the *fences* that controlled me for years:

*Fence:* You mustn't go to the county fair. That is being worldly and: *"you never know what that might lead to."*

*Fence:* Christians can't eat where they sell liquor. You might be tempted and drink a glass of wine: *"You never know what that might lead to, and you might become an alcoholic."*

*Fence:* Good Christians mustn't dance. If you hold each other you never know where that could end up: maybe kissing: *"You never know what that might lead to."*

*Fence:* Christians shouldn't drink wine. The Bible warns about drunkenness and wine could lead to becoming an alcoholic: *"You never know what that might lead to."*

Let's take a look at this last one. In Luke Jesus says, *"And take heed to yourselves, lest at any time your hearts be overcharged [weighted down or heavy] with surfeiting, drunkenness and the cares of this life and so that the day come upon you unawares"* (Luke 21:34-35). Now, let's read that again real slow. Does this mean I will burn in hell if I get caught in the cares of this life, begin to worry, or drink wine? Does that mean if I worry about anything I am going to hell?"

In this passage, Jesus talked about three things. First, what is surfeiting. It means gluttony or eating to excess. Now don't get under condemnation if you are overweight or on the other hand drinking a glass of wine while you are over eating. Why do many pastors preach on these two verses and leave out gluttony and the cares of this life? No condemnation to you but could it be most of us are so overweight that Satan tries to condemn us just by reading those scriptures. If you are overweight like me and don't know that there is no condemnation for Christians, then you might put up a *fence* to keep you from sinning. Remember the example from above: Christians can't eat where they sell liquor. You might be tempted to have a glass of wine and become an alcoholic.

Well if the above thinking is right, shouldn't we have this *fence:* Overweight Christians should not go to a cafeteria where they serve mashed potatoes, gravy, and rich creamy desserts.

You never know what that might lead to. If you go to a cafeteria, that might lead to being possessed by a spirit of gluttony. Your heart could be weighted down with clogged arteries and you'll gain weight. I know that sounds funny, but it is funny how we pick, and choose from a passage of scripture that we don't have a problem with and then use it to condemn others.

FEAR, FEAR, AND MORE FEAR!

Do you see the religious traditional *fences* the church builds? Do you feel and hear the fear in all of these demands? It is really a spirit of fear working in the church through a perverted message of grace mixed with legalism and is producing a toxic gospel. This has made the body of Christ sick. Thank God, "That by His strips we are healed and we can receive healing in our spiritual sickness" (1st Peter 2:24).

According to our Sunday rules, I couldn't do any kind of work. You couldn't cut the grass. You had to close your business down and couldn't do any kind of work. You had to put on those stiff Sunday clothes and go to Sunday school and church. There were so many rules for Sunday; all you could do is sit at home and wish for Monday. Even today the religiously correct mobs (gossips) will form against you and spurn your name as a heretic if you don't keep their Sunday traditions.

If you feel it is your obligation to attend church Sunday morning you are under church tradition law. If your attitude is, it is a pleasure to go to church Sunday; you are under New Covenant Grace. In other words, once you moved from the Old Covenant to the New Covenant, your law attitude is gone and now it's a pleasure to be a functioning Christian. God's Word is not a book of rules, but a book of His love letters. A Christian man gave me a rule one day: "Christians shouldn't go into places where they sell liquor."

Here is how I answered him. I knew he was talking about restaurants having a bar and I responded, "Then you would starve to death. Where do you buy your groceries?"

He said, "Kroger's."

"You know they sell liquor there don't you?" He got angry and left. One of the best ways to see if a person is under the stress of

Christian religion is this: start talking about the finished work of the Cross, the grace of God, and mention: *"He remembers our sins no more"* (Hebrews 8:12). If a person is bound, eventually they will get angry.

Here is some scriptural help for your Christian friends whom you believe are possibly trapped in legalistic religion.

If they say:

"You must confess your sins to get forgiveness."
Answer: *"He remembers our sins no more"* (Hebrews 8:12).

If they are trapped, you will hear a "*Yeah but*," and they will give you another scripture thus trying to prove the scripture you just quoted is a lie.

"God is judging the world with the weather."
Answer: When someone sees our Father as a judge and believe He is judging the world with storms, cyclones and earthquakes, quote this one to them: *"For God did not send His Son into the world to judge the world but that the world would be saved through Him"* (John 3:17).

For God to judge (kill) people in the world He would have to kill a lot of his own people, the church: His body. We would have to change the Lord's Prayer also to: Our Judge who art in heaven. Normal people never think about killing their own family, so why would God kill His own body through judgment?

**BUZZWORD 3**
(Mafia Wearing It)

Wearing it is showing off one's status in the organization by dressing the part which usually involves an Italian pinstriped suit and rich looking silk shirt. You would also notice a bright silk tie, a matching hankie in the breast pocket and a diamond pinky ring. Just above his ring a gold diamond bracelet and or a Rolex and matching gold cufflinks. When they walked into the party or night club, they expect to be seen and honored. They love statements like, "Hey Tony, I like that suit, nice Rolex. Where did you find that fox hanging on your arm?" Tony's ego is reinforced for the evening and now he is higher than when he snorted cocaine in his Mercedes.

Christian Religion Wearing It

Christian religion in churches proudly has a show of one's status by dressing the way headquarters says makes them look Holy. In the church I attended, women couldn't wear expensing clothes or gold jewelry, because that would be pride. Unlike Tony, men couldn't wear colored shirts or cufflinks because that would be flashy. Their deception was that holiness was from the *outside-in* rather than the *inside-out.*

The women had to wear long dresses and sleeves down to their wrists. Women were not permitted to shave under their arms so they had to keep their armpits covered. Women couldn't wear make-up unless they were in a casket. Most of the women looked better in the casket than they did in church. Oh yes, these are all *fences* to keep the church people from sinning thus making them think they look more Holy. Women can't wear pants or jeans because of the scripture that says:

*"Women are not to wear anything that pertaineth to a man."* (Deut. 22:5).

The above scripture was written to the Jews who were under the law. We are Gentiles and were never given the law, but if you really believe that is for you, and you take a trip to India where men wear dresses, then you couldn't wear any clothes at all. Now see how silly legalism can make us?

## BUZZWORD 4

(The Don or Boss)

The head of the Family who runs the show, and decides
who gets made and who gets *whacked.*

The Denominational Headquarters Don or Boss:
The head (don or boss) of a denomination is the one who calls the shots. He lays down the law (literally) from denominational traditions having been passed down for decades. He is the one who starts the ball rolling and decides which pastors, evangelists, bible teachers, or prophets are going to get *wacked* for not keeping with traditional teaching or breaking the Jewish Law. This is only one example among many others.

*"And so you cancel the word of God in order to hand down your own tradition"* (Mark 7:13).

When religious traditions rule, you will stress out trying to be religiously correct, thus destroying your peace and smile. It's been said that dogmatic religious traditions can make you angry and want to argue. The religious people trying to keep the rules are so right. I was so right if you looked at my face you could see that I was right; **dead** right—no joy or smiles. This is what I mean about the thief coming to *whack* and steal your peace and joy. How can a person be joyful if you believe God is a Mafia type Godfather sitting in heaven as a judge? He is not sitting up ready to *whack* you and cast you into hell.

He is not a Godfather sitting on a swivel chair in judgment. He is our Father God who loves us unconditionally. He does not ordain legalistic hit-men to stand behind pulpits with a legalistic machine gun. They rip God's family with bullets of fear by demanding we keep the Big Ten, the law, and church rules. Denominational church GODFATHERS ordain ministers who can preach rule-based doctrines for the purpose of control, again, many times unknowingly. God our Father anoints ministers to preach the unconditional love that is manifesting through His Son Jesus for the purpose of *freedom.*

♥ He is God our Father, who through His Son Jesus went to college, passed the exams and put the results in your file.

♥ Jesus ran in the Olympics won the gold and He hung it around your neck. The more you get to know Jesus, religious bondage with just fade.

When Jesus hung on the cross and cried out, "It is finished." He meant it and there is nothing that we must do to add to His finished work on the cross to *be* saved or *stay* saved. We choose to believe and accept what He said. Here is another one I had to have someone help me to misunderstand. The Pharisees asked Jesus what they must do to do the work of God, and he , Jesus answered,

"*The* work *of God is this: believe (trust) in the one he has sent*" (John 6:29).

Under law, you must ***do***, but under grace, it is Jesus plus nothing: ***done***. Oh yes, good works will follow but not because of a law or church rules, but because of an inner desire to do good works;

"*His yoke it easy His burden in light*" (Matthew 11:30).

Again, did you notice He went from their question of "works" in the plural to "work" in the singular? The yoke of Grace is easy and Jesus came that we would have His Life inside us, which means (freedom from religious works that produce worry, anxiety, and depression). But hit-men behind pulpits will many times pull out their legalistic machine guns and say it is Jesus plus, tithing, volunteering, not missing church, not wearing makeup, not drinking wine, and the list goes on with many other rules.

## DRINKING TOXIC COCKTAILS

You cannot merge a living Jesus with a dead Moses. Moses is dead, and we are dead to the Law of Moses. In other words, you can't mix the Law with grace (Jesus). Mixing law and grace is a toxic cocktail and it poisons everyone who drinks it. Have you been drinking poison? Have you been poisoned by the lies of religion? This is the point I want to make: You died to the power of the law when you died with Christ. That old man (old nature) is what died with Jesus on the Cross. Now, we are one with Christ whom God raised from the dead. As a result, God is producing a harvest of good deeds through us. His acceptance, and our continued salvation, is contingent on grace alone. Religious activity such as a set of church rules or the Ten Commandments is all flesh:

*"The flesh profits nothing"* (John 6:63).

God loves and accepts you just like you are just because of what His Son did at the cross not what you do or don't do. God sent His Son Jesus to pay for your sins. They are already forgiven; past, present and future. All you have to do is accept His forgiveness by faith: choosing to believe.

*"For God so loved the world (that is you) that He gave His only Son, that whoever believes in Him shall not perish, but have everlasting LIFE. For He did*

*not send His Son into the world to judge the world but that the world would be saved through Him"* (John 3:16-17).

> *"He who has the Son (living in him) has the life of the Son. He, who has not the Son, has not His life"* (1st. John 5:12)

In other words, batteries were not included when you were born out of your mother's womb. If you have not accepted His forgiveness, make this simple statement aloud and mean it in your heart: **"God in Heaven, I am a sinner, and I accept you and receive your forgiveness of my sins right now. I choose to believe that Jesus is now my Lord because of your grace. Holy Spirit, I receive my right to life now."**

> *"If you confess with your mouth that Jesus is Lord and believe in your heart that God raised him from the dead, you will be saved. For it is by believing in your heart that you are made right with God, and it is by confessing with your mouth that you are saved"* (Romans 10:9-10).

If you accepted what Jesus did earlier in life, and you have been taught you have failed God, and He has swiveled His chair and turned His back on you, I have good news: He is still your Father. Pray this with me: **"My Father, I am so glad that I know the truth now. I have been taught lies and now I know you have not left or turned you back on me. Jesus thank you I am a believer and still saved."**

Thank him that you are as saved as ever and ask Him to show you Jesus, the message of grace that walked the earth.

I know you have many questions. Feel free to email me anytime: tommyhawk@live.com / tommyhawkministries.com

# 7

# REMEMBERING

**Remembering:** *"Dad and forgiving him"*

I hated dad so much I did not want to carry his name. When I entered the country music business, this was a perfect time to change it. I regret it now because I realize how much that hurt him. Sad to say, but if you remember earlier, I described him as a tyrant who beat mother with his fists and cut the blood out of us kids with tree limbs. We would have to cut our own switches from a tree or bush. For those of you who do not know what a switch is, it is a slim branch of a tree or bush about three feet long.

When dad beat us, he would go into a rage swinging the switch. Sometimes I would take my knife and ring it, which means, cutting a real thin line around it in a couple of places so it would break with a couple of swings. Periodically, he would cut his own and we would have welts and cuts on our bodies for weeks because of continual whippings. My mother would step in, and he would turn and use it on her. I remember one time after a whipping; he smashed her in the face with his fist for getting involved. I thought of getting the gun and shooting him.

There are three reasons I am sharing about my dad. First, I am hoping I can paint a picture of an earthly father who was very different from my Heavenly Father who I am still getting to know. Our Father in heaven is not a Godfather - type waiting for you mess up so He can punish with a switch and then damn you to hell. He is not a child abuser like dad, but our loving Father who gave His only Son on that Cross to pay for our sins: past, present and future.

*"The death he died, he died to sin once for all [SIN]; past, present and future sins, but the life he lives, he lives to God"* (Romans 6:10 brackets and emphasis mine).

Secondly, I want you to know that I forgave him before the bitterness destroyed me. I was lying in bed this morning regretting my bitterness. Even though I was remembering my sin against dad, Jesus was not remembering my sins or bitterness's.

Thirdly, I am hoping you will understand why it has been so hard for me, and possibly you, to accept our loving Heavenly Father as our daddy. (*Some even use the tender Aramaic term "Abba" for God, which loosely translates to "daddy"*). If you have or had a parent like mine and are having the same problems, I believe my writings can give you the hope of knowing God our Father as a loving Daddy, Papa or Abba.

I was in New York speaking at a Full Gospel Business Men's Convention, and after returning home, I was surprised to see dad was at my house. We conversed a while about my trip and then I put a tape in the player so he could listen to my life story that was taped in New York. There was a section that I did not want him to hear, but he heard it. I made this statement on the tape: "I don't remember dad or mother putting their arms around me and telling me they loved me or were proud of me." I felt so bad that dad heard that, so I reached and turned off the player and tried to change the subject. Then he said something that changed my whole attitude toward Him and brought me to forgiveness. He said, "Son do you remember your grandpa hugging you or telling you how proud he was of you?" My mind flashed back as I remembered him telling me about his dad whipping him with a horsewhip. Wow, with tears filling my eyes, I understood why he treated us kids and mother the way he did. What he experienced with his dad was all he knew about marriage and raising a family.

I remember when he accepted Jesus as his savior, there was a major change in his actions toward our family. I also remember the day that Jesus spoke to me, "Go visit your dad and seek his forgiveness."

My response: "Jesus, he is the one who owes me an apology!" I really didn't want to do what Jesus told me to do. However, within a few weeks; I went to his house to visit. At the right time, I said, "Dad, I want you to know that I've been bitter toward you for many years." "I know that, son," dads responded.

"I am asking you to forgive me," I said. I didn't say another word.

He remained quiet.

I stayed quiet for a few minutes. With my heart busting with rejection, I returned to my car and headed down the highway with tears as evidence of more hurt. With tears flowing down my cheeks, I said, "Jesus, I expected him to at the least say he was sorry. Jesus, he never admitted one wrong thing he had ever done to me, mother, or my siblings."

"Don't be concerned with his response; you did what I asked you to do," Jesus responded.

As I continued down the highway, tears streaming down my face, hurting and suffering again. I stopped, bent over my steering wheel; I started screaming out for answers: "Lord, will dad ever affirm me and give me any father-son encouragement?"

"You are free!" Jesus responded.

Even though I left his house upset, I am sure he did forgive me. I forgave dad and that freed me from bitterness to this day.

The truth of Grace (Jesus) makes you free from bitterness. Once you understand how much you were forgiven, it just becomes natural to forgive others. We do not forgive to get forgiveness, which was under the Old Covenant Law. Under the New Covenant, we forgive as we have received forgiveness: no conditions. We just *freely* pass on what we have *freely* received from Jesus.

*"Be kind to each other, tenderhearted, forgiving one another, just as God through Christ has forgiven you"* (Ephesians 4:32 NLT, emphasis mine).

Mother divorced dad, then he married Thelma a few years later, and the abuse was the same with her as it was with mother. Dad had become a Christian, but he was still in bondage to anger, which is a sign of suffering rejection. Thelma's' son revealed that dad almost beat her to death. Even as mean as dad was, I still miss him and regret my resentment and bitterness. If you have a dad or mother still living, if possible, spend time with them. You don't get a second chance to enjoy them. Dad loved to watch the Cincinnati Reds on television, and I now regret that I never took him to a game. Don't do as I did and end up with regrets. Satan will use that regret as a landing strip for guilt and condemnation later on in life.

I did many things to dad out of bitterness and resentment. I wanted to hurt him for the way he rejected me and hurt my mother.

I regret it now that we spent the holidays with mother because of my bitterness toward him. I actually damaged my son through my bitterness. I refused to let his grandpa see him until he was five years old. My wife slipped behind my back and let him see Shaun, and now I am glad she did. Part of the reason I hated him so much, I picked up (unknowingly) mother's resentment and bitterness toward him. I had the same attitude toward him that mother had. Unknowingly, she contributed to destroying our relationship. Just make sure you do not let that happen to you, because you will regret it, and Satan will use it against you for years.

Now, for you personally, is it going well for you? If your life is unstable, stressed and depressed, check your *attitude* concerning your parents, friends, and family.

*"Honor your father and mother that it may go well with you and that you may enjoy long life on the earth"* (Ephesians 6:2-3).

Life is short; spend *time* with your parents, kids and grandkids. *Remember they need you more than they do the things you buy them.* In my opinion, the most important thing for kids is they see Jesus in you. Oh yes, as you can see by reading my life story, I have made many mistakes with my family. However, the greatest legacy I will leave them is, they know that I know Jesus and that He is my very life! Through all our mistakes, aren't you glad for this scripture?

*"He remembers our sin NO more"* (Hebrews 8:12).

Concluding my remembrance of dad, I want to end on a positive note. He is with Jesus now, and I don't have to tell you that life is short. It just seems like yesterday that I was home working in the tobacco fields, suckering, spudding, and hanging it in the barn. Knowing my grandpa as I did, I can only imagine what dad went through as a young boy. I really doubt that his dad ever affirmed him. Coming from a man who learned to hate his dad, please don't make the same mistake that I did with either of your parents, family or friends. I wish I could have gotten to know him. After I started traveling as a Bible teacher-preacher, I was sitting at his house one day and we were talking about God's Word. Then he shocked me with this statement. "I never thought I would have son that would be a preacher." That statement shook me to the bone. I could hardly hold back the tears. This was the only time in my life I felt dad's love. To me that was a word of *affirmation* and being proud of me. I know that Jesus inspired him to say that.

**Remembering:** *"Freddie's Casket"*

As I stood over my brother's casket, I spoke these words: "I will take up where you left off." Little did I know where those words would lead me. I have traveled over 30 years sharing God's unconditional love. My travels have taken me many places, including The Full Gospel Business Men's Fellowship Conferences (FGBMFI), television programs such as The 700 Club and Trinity Broadcasting Network (TBN). Like Freddie and the Apostle Paul, my passion is to know Jesus intimately.

*"My determined purpose is, that I may know Him: that I may progressively become more deeply and intimately acquainted with Him"* (Philippians 3:10 AMP).

I remember a man telling me a story about Freddie working under his truck. As he walked by, he bent over and asked, "Fred, who are you talking to?" He said, "I am talking to Jesus, because when I am talking to Him, Satan can't get a word in edgewise."

*"Be cheerful no matter what; pray all the time;* [without-ceasing] *thank God no matter what happens. This is the way God wants you who belong to Christ Jesus to live"* (1st. Thess. 5:16-18, brackets mine).

He prayed without ceasing. I never forgot that because he was practicing the scripture above.

His daughter Angie said, "My remembrance of him was sitting in his rocking chair in the corner of the room, reading the Bible. The Sunday before his death, he preached at our church. They asked him to preach again next Sunday, and he said, 'If I'm still living.' Well, we know how that went. Looking back, the greatest attribute I saw in daddy was his hunger to know God. His joyful relationship with God has helped me become a joyful person."

I have already shared this story about Freddie; However, I want to remind you again. This was the last time I saw him alive and that is the reason I am bringing this up again. I was traveling all over the country singing country music, and it was on Christmas or Thanksgiving break. I was at my mother's house in Gallipolis, and Freddie walked in, came over to me, bent down and hugged me. He said some words that I never heard from anyone in my family or any church people. He said, "Hey brother, I love you, you know that don't you?" Neither on mother or dad's side of the family had I ever heard those words come over anyone's lips. Through those words, God planted a desire in me to know how much He loves me. Since Jesus has written 66 love stories, I figured those letters were the best place for me to start. I have averaged two to five hours daily in His love letters since Freddie went home. I have spent hundreds of hours reading and talking to Jesus, just like Freddie under his truck.

I love you Freddie! See you soon.

**Remembering:** *"Mother and forgiven her"*

Mother was a great cook and worked hard, although there were never any satisfactory words of appreciation ever given to her from dad. This taught me to compliment my wife through the years and try to make her feel appreciated. If dad ever gave her a good word, most of the time it was because he wanted sex. I knew many times she was satisfying him sexually just to get him to treat me better. I know many times that sex would buy me dad's car to use on Saturday night. I know she felt more like the home prostitute rather than a wife. The way he treated her turned me bitter and the evidence that I hated him was in the way I talked to him after I was of age. For years, I resented everything he stood for and did many things to get even, including letting my hair grow long. I found you could lose your peace of mind and eventually your health by trying to get even.

Mother married George, who was a gambler, alcoholic, and very dangerous to be around when he was drunk. If he was under the influence and you crossed him, he would kill you. Everyone loved

George when he was not drinking. You probably remember Pat in chapter one, having an affair with mother in the woods. After mother had told George about this, he threatened to kill him many times. Mother told me one day that he was gone for a long time and when he walked in the door she said, "His face was red as a beet and he looked like he was scared. I have never seen him look like that. He spent a long time in the bathroom washing his hands. That was the day I believed he murdered him."

They found Pat's body in a grape vineyard in West Virginia a few days later. After this, she told me that he asked her many times if God forgives murder. She told him Jesus paid for all our sins. After those words, George did become a believer in Jesus. George admitted to her before he died that he killed him. Mother said that when he died, there was a smile and a look of surprise on his face as he was leaving his body.

Mother made many mistakes and had a hard life suffering from rejection from her family, dad, and then George. She gave birth to five kids and had four on the bottle at the same time. I forgave her for what I witnessed in the woods when I was young. A mother's adultery is a major setback for a son. In a son's eyes, a mother never does wrong. My rejection came from all sides while growing up. I guess I was bitter at both of my parents but didn't want to admit mother's mistakes.

**REMEMBERING:** *"Building my own prison"*

Satan is a brick, block, and mortar provider. Being hurt without forgiving each of the offenders was a brick or a block in building my wall. Satan will help you build a wall by reminding you of what they did to you. If you want to build a wall around you, he will supply all the mean people you will need. It all started in grade school when my family and the kids at school would reject me. Because of fear, I became a loner. I would avoid and block my offenders from communication. When I became self-centered, it was easy to build my own prison because every rejection was just another block or brick for my wall. It was not long before I had built a wall around me. Yes, I built it! My mother would always make sure we were clean and our hair combed neatly. As soon as I would get on the bus, Doug would make fun of me and always mess up my hair before I would get to school. He always threatened us kids, and we all grew to hate him.

As I write this, I can still see the snarl on his lips, hate on his face, and the look of disgust in his eyes for me. As I continued to realize how much Jesus had forgiven me, it not only became easy to forgive Doug, but also to pray for him. I actually saw him a few years ago, and I looked at him without hate.

Rejected people will reject people. Once I had my wall built, I withdrew from everyone except Monvil. Even though Monvil was my friend, I would not let him come inside my wall. It was hard to communicate with me because of the fear of not being accepted. It was safe behind the wall because no one could really get to me. After I became a Christians and began to understand God's grace and His unconditional love, forgiving through the years has become easier. When I chose to release everyone who had rejected me, I realized that I was in prison. I was inside the wall that I had been constructing for years. It was lonely behind that wall, and no one could break through except the love of Jesus.

I have had people say, "Tommy, what would have happened if you had gone to family members or a pastor for help?" That is a great question, and I will write more about it in my next book: *Billy Goat Religion.* However, legalistic family members, church people and pastors with that holier-than-thou *attitude,* were the worst when it came to rejecting me. Preaching the law and church rules brought rejection that is indescribably depressing because you can never live up to religions standards. Religion has been harder to get free from than the Mafia, because the standards are always being raised.

Every wall built, comes from unforgiveness. The blocks or bricks must have mortar to hold them together. In the spiritual sense, the cement or mortar is fear, and I could not escape. Satan also supplied all the mortar I needed for my wall. My fears (mortar) held the blocks together, and the result: I had built my own prison. It was lonely, yet safe behind that wall. I could not open up and be honest with anyone or invite anyone into my new home because I hid my depression there. I found great freedom in this scripture:

*"For God has not given us a spirit of fear"* (2 Timothy 1:7).

Another question I am always asked is this: "How did you get the wall down?" That is like asking me how I got out of the Mafia, in a few words. As fear controls those in the Mafia, it also controls legalistic, unforgiving, and bitter people. I was so bitter at dad; it was easy for that bitterness and hatred to continue for other people. I just could not forgive the ones who rejected me. I cannot answer the question above completely in a couple of statements. However, the answer is in the scripture above, and in this one:

*"Such love has no fear, because perfect love expels all fear [mortar]. If we are afraid, it is for fear of punishment, and this shows that we have not fully experienced the perfect love of Jesus"* (1 John 4:18 NLT, emphasis mine).

In other words, fear is a spirit, a real being that you cannot see with your physical eyes. The love of Jesus is perfect, and once you began to see how much He loves you, the mortar in the wall cracks and crumbles. Therefore, the answer is just getting to know Jesus. The results will be freedom from fear.

When I believed that God was a type of GODFATHER rather than God, our loving Father, it was hard to get out of my own prison. Are you a prisoner and want to be free? Get a legal pad and ask His Holy Spirit to bring every name of the people you need to forgive. Speak each name aloud. Example: Aloud, "I forgive Kevin."

and then Cross his name out. Write down the date when you forgave that person because the accuser (Satan) will come back and tell you that you are still bitter at that person. Then you take him to your legal pad and show him the date you forgave Kevin. As you do this, you will receive great freedom, and His peace will overtake you and heal your emotions.

*"By His wounds you are healed"* (1 Peter 2:24).

**Remembering**: *"Malcolm Smith"*
www.unconditionallovefellowship.com

I was in New York speaking at a Full Gospel Business Men's Convention, and after the meeting, I was asked to come visit a home and minister to a couple with marriage problems. As I was leaving their house, they asked, "Have you heard of Malcolm Smith?" They handed me a tape series entitled, "Love One Another." I had never heard of him, but I had been studying the love of God for about ten years and was really looking forward to the tapes. A couple of days later, on my way back to Ohio, I put in the first tape and Malcolm made a statement right at the beginning that got my attention. What he said startled and then angered me. However, later that seed grew, and changed my toxic understanding of God's love.

Here is what he said: "You cannot do anything or stop doing anything to increase or decrease God's love for you. His love is unconditional and He does not love you because you read your Bible, go to church, or try to keep church rules. He loves you because of who He is, not because of who you are."

My thoughts: "This man is a heretic preaching doctrines of demons!" I have to continue tithing, reading my bible, going to church, and obeying the rules. I cannot drink wine or curse, because God is watching and listening to me.

Christian Religion taught me if we did not walk that straight and narrow path, which in their eyes was keeping the church rules and obeying the Ten Commandments, and if we did not obey, we would fall from Grace, lose our salvation, and set off on a path to hell. We had to go to the altar and beg God to forgive us every Sunday. At that time, I did not know it was fear grabbing me. I was scared as I listened to Malcolm teaching this strange doctrine, so I turned off the tape. According to what Malcolm was saying, we do not have to perform to be favored or accepted.

We had to wear our Sunday smiley masks when we went to church. We had to whisper in church, sit up straight, hug old people who had bad breath, and answer all their religious questions like, "Have you been to the altar lately asking God to forgive your daily sins?" I always wondered: "If I have to confess my sin for forgiveness, what if I forget one?"

Here is a good question for you to ponder: If Jesus paid for all your sins on the Cross, why do you have to confess your sins to get forgiveness? We confess our sin in agreement with God that it was sin, and then thank Him for paying for that sin two thousand years ago. Sin is gratifying a legitimate God giving desire in an illegitimate way.

At the end of each service was the dreaded altar call. Some religious person with a look of disgust for sinners would stroll back and forth across the wooden floor. They would grab your hand, as if to shake hands and then drag you down the aisle to the altar. The floor had black scuffmarks from the resistance of sinners in the hands of an ANGRY saint. Ha! I figured God had to be angry like dad and the religious people I knew. They would take your hand as if to shake hands and then at the same time ask, "Would you like to get saved?" Sunday was such a dreary day; we could hardly wait until Monday to be ourselves again.

If you did not keep the church rules, you were in rebellion and going to hell. I heard a pretty well-known preacher in a big church say, "If you don't tithe, you are going to hell." Many believe they cannot drink Coke out of a bottle because it looks too much like a beer bottle, so they have to pour it in a glass. Yes, I know, it is shocking. Even though I was in fear listening to Malcolm, down deep inside there was a hope that he was telling the truth. I turned the tape back on and fear gripped me again. I did not know that it was a Jezebel religious spirit of fear.

If you can remember one thing, this will help you in your Christian walk: Just believe by faith that God's love is unconditional, and He never corrects you with fear. However, I was experiencing so much fear listening to Malcolm, I was about to pitch the tape out the window. Then he made a statement that was the deciding factor in my decision to stay in ministry. The result was the beginning of getting free from Christian "religion." Here is what he said:

"Whatever you believe, is it working?

If it is not, then there is something you believe that is an error or a lie."

I shouted out, "Oh Jesus, I just heard your voice through this man." What I believed was not working. I was not walking or enjoying my Christian life because there was no peace of mind. I was always struggling in performance to please God. I had never heard that God's love was unconditional. Then it hit me! Wow! I can't lose my salvation! My salvation came without good works! If works do not save me, then I do not continue to be saved by good works. I mean, it was a "DUH" … even God doesn't take back a gift.

*"For it is by grace you have been saved, through faith and this is not from yourselves; it is the* ***gift*** *of God"* (Ephesians 2:8, emphasis mine).

Christian religion blinded me to this wonderful truth of unconditional love. This is where many Christians are living today; unaware that God's gift of love is unconditional. Many are still in bondage to the traditional beliefs of their organized church. Maybe you are also struggling to keep the Jewish law, the Ten

Commandments and or church rules. This can be depressing, and the result is bondage to fear. I had been walking by fear, rather than by faith. The religion of performance (*trying* rather than *trusting*) is a walk by fear and the result is stress. Fear will cause you to perform to keep God on your side. Understanding unconditional love (Grace) will delete the mortar from your wall. It has taken years of listening to Malcolm Smith and many other Grace preachers to get all the mortar to crumble and to break free from Christian religion.

Getting free from the Mafia happened more quickly than getting free from Mafia-type religiously correct Christian religion. The mortar (fear) began to disintegrate and the wall began to *crumble* and *tumble* as Malcolm Smith taught me the unconditional love of God. His teaching of this scripture:

*"There is no fear in love. But perfect love drives out fear, because fear has to do with punishment. The one who fears is not made perfect in love"* (1 John 4:18).

**Remembering:** "*Blacklick Woods*"

Blacklick Woods is place where I go to pray. This day was special. It was a beautiful autumn day, squirrels were preparing for winter, and birds were singing a welcome to the beautiful colors of autumn. I was kicking leaves and clowning around with Jesus. I looked up to the heavens, there was a slight warm breeze, leaves flying in my face, and I pointed my finger and said to Him, in a fun, got-you attitude: "Jesus, there is one thing I know you can't do. I was involved with the Mafia, a drug addict, close to being an alcoholic, and I am still a sinner, and you can't change my *past*."

He is so cool. As a squirrel went across my path, He said, "Really! First, you do not have that *past*. Your old *past* has *passed*. My past is now yours. Your identity (new nature) is not a sinner anymore, because that (old nature) is what died with Me on the Cross— that was your old sin nature. You *were* by nature a sinner but *now* you are righteous because you have my nature.

If you are a Christian and have an alcohol problem, never tell anyone that you are an alcoholic. Your identity is a child of God with an alcohol problem, or if you told a lie and someone calls you a liar, do not accept it. Your identity is not a liar, but a child of God who may have told a lie. Your identity is now a Saint who does sin but He paid for all of them, *past*, *present*, and *future*.

*"He remembers your sins no more"* (Hebrews 8:12).

Concerning the above scripture, I remember a true story about a Catholic woman who kept telling all the women that Jesus was talking to her. The Ladies went to the Priest and told him what Sara had been telling them. Then, the Priest called Sara in and said, "I have been hearing some strange stories about how God has been talking to you."

Sara nodded and said, "Yes, He has Father."

"Well Sara, I want you to ask Him something the next time He talks to you. Ask Him what sins I confessed to Him yesterday."

She said, "Okay" and left.

Toward the end of the week, Sara came back and told the Priest that Jesus had spoken to her again. He said, "Did you ask him about the sin I confessed to Him last week?"

"Yes, I did."

"Well Sara, what did He say?" Sara looked the Priest right in the eyes and said, "He told me He did not remember."

**Remembering:** *"The guard rail and my encounter with Jesus"*

Gallipolis, Ohio is just across the river from Point Pleasant, WV. This is where the motion picture, The Mothman Prophecies, was filmed. This is where the Silver Bridge also fell into the Ohio River back in the 1960's.

I remember my encounter with God's Love that night in 1977. A few months had passed, and I was driving that same road, headed toward Gallipolis. I remembered a white guardrail on the right side of my car where I stopped. When I reached the same place, I pulled over a second time and looked up through my glass roof just to give thanks and reminisce. As I looked up this time, I saw a big Cross on top of this hill beside the highway. I did not notice it the first time. I was there again about eleven o'clock in the evening, and there it was: a huge Cross glowing from the bright spotlights shining on it. Then it hit me again! I really did have an encounter with Jesus at the foot of a Cross. I wept again, and even now, I am writing this with tears flowing. I remember the song we used to sing in the Old Big Four Country Church: "At the Cross, at the Cross, where I first saw the light."

I am getting to know the love that Jesus manifested that night; I've found out that He is not like a Godfather, with iron-fisted power to control. He is not a child abuser, but a lover of His Children whom He created. He does not call you to church altars today. He says, "Come to the Cross." I do not give altar calls anymore because that was Old Covenant, and it was a place of shedding of animal blood: Death. Today the altar in the church is a place of making promises, new commitments, and pledges to obey the Big Ten or church rules. I give "Cross calls" today, and this produces life. The spotless blood of Jesus was shed on the Cross, once and for all our sins: past, present and future; a call to (life), not a call to (sacrifice).

**REMEMBERING: "***My children: Shaun and Charity*"

Shaun and Charity, you are so special, and I am so very proud of you. I am so sorry for the grief and hurt you have experienced because of divorce. The pinnacle of all my rejections and regrets was divorce. As the Mafia would say, "I feel *whacked*." I really do understand what you have been through and are going through. I went through the same thing when I was young, and I am still suffering from my parents' divorce. I know the pain and insecurity that emotional suffering produces when a family splits. Parents, please don't let the children convince you that they understand and accept their mother and dad divorcing. I had hope that dad and mother would get back together right up until dad passed. Getting to know Jesus has kept me sane and this scripture has been prophetic for me through the years:

*"I will never leave you; never will I forsake you"* (Hebrew 13:5).

**REMEMBERING:** *"I could write another book remembering my best friend"*

I thank you for all the times you have kept me alive when death knocked on my door. Thank you for saving my life when I overdosed on cocaine in Florida. You took me back to my house, even though I had no idea how I got there. Thank you for saving my life from a deadly crash in Ft. Lauderdale, and many others.

I remember when my flight to Charlotte was in trouble and You took charge of the airplane. Thank you for a praying wife that saved my life in a deadly crash in Milledgeville, GA. Thank you for giving me two wonderful children and grandchildren. Thank you for always encouraging me in Blacklick Woods as I brought my depression and anxieties to you.

Thank you for showing me the message of Grace and unconditional acceptance. Your love letters keep reminding me that you are a person who loves me and understands all my rejections, pressures, and attacks from Satan. When you speak, I always remember it, and the place.

I remember what you told me as I was traveling through West Virginia many years ago. You said: *"I will never leave or forsake you"* (Hebrews 13:5).

When You spoke those words, I was a newborn Christian and did not know those were in the Bible. Oh Jesus, how many times remembering these words has comforted me! There are no conditions for me to meet in those words. Through all of my study in Your Word, You have gifted me as a teacher. Now I get to teach

Your love letters to anyone who wants to know You.

**Remembering: "Tony"**

As I was finishing writing my story, my friend Tony went home to be with Jesus in March 2013 at the age of 98. I sure do miss him. He was like a dad to me, and we spent many hours in the recording studio mixing country music to our taste. When we would get it right, Tony would throw up his hands in an Italian gesture and say something exciting in Italian. Tony was also a great cook and could have been a great chef. I understand He had fifteen different recipes for Spaghetti, and he gave me his secret one that very few people have. I never liked spaghetti; however, years ago Tony and I got on my bus and headed to Philadelphia to meet with Mike Douglas, who was a major talk show host at that time. Tony started cooking spaghetti sauce on the bus. After about four hours cooking his sauce, the aroma was really making me hungry. Finally, he put in the Italian sausage and cooked it in the sauce about another hour. Man, was I getting hungry. That Italian bread was baking in the oven and it reminded me of the Celebrity Hotel in Cleveland! Finally, I stopped the bus at a roadside park and we started eating, it was so good. I am not kidding you, that was the best spaghetti and Italian sausage meal I have ever had. I know Tony would be happy about me sharing his recipe with my friends. Therefore, if you request the recipe and send any gift to our ministry, I will send it to you.

**HE IS COMING BACK:**

Our fulfillment (Jesus) is coming back soon. Depending on this world's pleasures for fulfillment will cause you to suffer from loneliness and depression. The world system: 666 - man - man - man, has nothing that can ever bring ongoing satisfaction. If that is where you are, do not run to religion or a preacher, unless he preaches the Cross of Jesus. Do you feel rejected? Run to Jesus; He will comfort you. Have you ever seen a black hearse pulling a U-Haul? As we get closer to going home, we realize that nothing this world has to offer satisfies. Oh, if we could only learn this in our younger years, we would understand that only Jesus satisfies, and is everything we are looking for. For some people, like me, it took many years to get that understanding.

Whatever problems you are going through, Jesus does not HAVE the answer. He IS the answer. This is all you really need to know concerning your future: Just get to know Jesus. We will see Him soon.

**WARNING**: Never let any preacher, bible teacher or pastor put you under the Old Covenant Law. Tell them you are not a Jew but a Gentile. The most deceiving trap of Satan is to get you in bondage to denominational rules, regulations or The Law. We are now in the New Covenant message of Grace and you are free to be you, not what religion wants you to be.

**Now this is a special word to my readers from Jesus.**

"I love you so much that I gave my Son to pay for your sin. My love for you held Me on the Cross, not the nails. I shed my blood through Jesus, for you, so just trust Me. No matter what the circumstance, trust me. As I have told the author of this book, 'I will never leave or forsake you' I am NOW giving you that same encouragement. If you knew how much I love you, there would never be any fear in your life. Get to know Me, experience my love, and watch the fears fade away. No matter what you go through in your time on earth, I am there breathing the breath of life IN you, THROUGH you, and AS you. You are saved, loved and accepted just the way you are. When you need to talk, come and open your heart and speak freely. I promise I will never judge, reject, or condemn you. I love you, you know that don't you?"

Jesus

## A SPECIAL WORD CONCERNING THIS BOOK:

It has been over a year since Jesus told me to write this book. I have revealed life situations that my family and close friends do not know. I also could write another book describing the hell I have been through while writing the manuscript. The feeling of being alone in this venture has been challenging to say the least. The scripture that I have quoted many times has brought me through; *"I will never leave or forsake you."*

The first half of this book is for the unsaved. That is the reason I put the word Mafia on the cover instead of a Cross. When you mention Mafia, you have everyone's attention. You should be shrewd, and take advantage of this book and give copies to your loved ones for Christmas and birthdays.

This is a great fishing tool. Go now my family, and preach the Gospel through this book.

"*Look, I am sending you out as sheep among wolves. So be as wise (shrewd) as snakes and harmless as doves*" (Matthew 10:16).

I would love to hear from you.
Tommy Hawk
Box 455, Reynoldsburg, Ohio 43068
www.tommyhawkministries.com / tommyhawk@live.com

# IN MEMORY

I dedicate the book in memory of a very special man who saved my life by freeing me from the grip of the Mafia. If you had the pleasure of meeting him, it would have been a great experience. Tony was one of the most loving, giving, amazing, and moral men I have ever known. He had a heart as big as the moon and could have been a millionaire and a major figure in the underworld, but his love for people hindered him.

In Cleveland and around the world, everyone who knew Tony loved him and said he was a trustworthy and loyal man. Many Hollywood Stars like Elvis and Phyllis Diller knew him. He spent three years with Elvis in Germany and Phyllis was one of his closest friends. For some of you old timers, Tony managed The Poni-Tails and helped to make Jim Stafford's big record, "Spiders and Snakes." In 1974, Mayor Perk of Cleveland, OH scheduled Tommy Hawk and His Warriors for the New Year's Eve party. The mayor scheduled us just because he trusted Tony. I went to see him at a senior home in the in 2010. He hardly knew me, and it crushed my heart. He was 98 when he left this world in 2013.

I sure do miss you Tony.

# FAMILY DEDICATION

*Shelia,* a true Gem: You gave me two beautiful children, taught me a lot about loving them and people. You are a loving Mother and Grandmother. Your future is bright.

*Shaun & Charity:* You are my pride and joy. I am so thankful that God blessed me with you. This scripture is for the both of you. "*Don't love money; be satisfied with what you have. For God has said, I will never fail you. I will never abandon you*" (Hebrews 13:5 NLT).

*Shaun*: When I hear people comment about you, I get so prideful. You are the only Bible that many people have and will ever read. Your calling in life is bright and your best years are ahead of you. God is setting you up to succeed, and equipping you every day for His purpose no matter what you go through. (Philippians 4:13).

*Charity*: Your name fits you so well. Having you as my daughter causes me to swell with pride also. When I am out in public, many times people come up to me and asked, "Do you know Charity Hawk?" When I tell them who I am, they light up like a candle. Because *Charity* never fails, you can never fail (ultimately). "*Love never fails*" (1st. Cor. 13:8). People who love most get hurt the most. So remember, God "*causes all things to work together for your good*" (Romans 8:28).

*GRAND KIDS*

*Lyric & Lleyton:* My awesome grandchildren: You both are very special to Grandpa. After I am gone, you will want to know where

Grandpa's heart was and what he believed. From Jesus, "I want you to know Me, I will never leave or forsake you." This book is a special dedication to the both of you.

*Lyric*: Your intelligence and ability to comprehend is a gift from Jesus. In your quest for understanding, just get to know Jesus. Everything else has no lasting satisfaction. "*People who know their God shall prove themselves strong and shall stand firm and do exploits for God*" Daniel 11:32).

*Lleyton*: You will be a great leader. Your awesome mind and determination will bring you before great people. Always focus on integrity in dealing with your peers. "*Be strong and courageous*" (Joshua 1:1-17).

# LETTERS OF APPRECIATION

Many Christians do not realize that preaching Jesus is ministering His love and it brings emotional healing and many times physical healings. I received this email from Pastor Armando in Brazil. He was in a meeting when I was teaching God's unconditional love.

Tom Autry who was traveling with me, and as he was singing and ministering on the keyboard, the students were weeping all over the Bible College, as God's love was manifesting in people though out the building.

I remember a man named Armando and another named Carlos who was weeping so loud you could sense the emotional healing was that was taking place in them and many others. I received this email today Nov. 19, 2011. As you read this, just ask His Holy Spirit to make His love real in you today. If you will, God is going to touch your emotions also.

* * *

Hello Man of God;

Here is what I remember from your meeting at World Harvest Bible College. On that day, I went to school just believing God for a special touch of his power and love. At that time my father was separated from my mom, and going through a divorce and it was hard for us to see such a man of God like my father do that. I also had moments to wonder, "Could I really be used by God the way it had been prophesied to me many times?" I remember mom and daddy telling me, "You are called from the womb to preach the gospel."

Your ministry that day at World Harvest Bible College marked my life when you ministered. You spoke about how God's love ministers; deliverance from fear, heals our emotions, and gives us an easy yoke. All I remember is that the anointing was so powerful in such a mighty way and the spirit of God began to overshadow me in such a way I felt like I was melting in His presence. Overwhelmed with His love, I couldn´t help but weep as I felt the love of Jesus. His sufferings and the price he paid for me became real and that love gave me hope. As you said, "Faith works by Love" I was encouraged and immediately had faith that I could do anything. Emotionally healed in the middle of that anointing of love, I knew God loved me and I was ready to go preach.

Tommy, NO words can express the love I felt that day. I just didn´t want that moment to end. I will never forget the song Tom Autry was singing: "Fill my cup Lord, I lift it up Lord, come and quench the thirst of my soul, bread of heaven fill me until I want no more, fill my cup fill it up and make me whole."

Wow praise God, as I am now writing this November. 18, 2011, I feel His Holy Spirit here in Brazil. My God, this is bringing me great memories right now as I have tears filling my eyes, thank you Jesus. Wow, I feel him right now, can´t stop weeping. I felt angels all over that Bible College in Ohio. The glory of God (His Love) was manifested at World Harvest Bible College and it has been 15 years ago. May God continue to anoint you with His love in spreading the power (the love of Jesus Christ) bringing great emotional healing to humanity.

Pastor Armando Penha
Brazil

* * *

Here is what some other pastors have shared with me:

## JAMES ROBINSON EVANGELISTIC ASSOCIATION

I am writing this letter in behalf of Tommy Hawk Ministries. I have worked with Tommy on several occasions and have found him to be a true servant of the Lord. His zeal and love is a tremendous blessing. I would recommend involvement in his ministry of love to anyone. I know he will be a blessing to your life.

*James Robinson*
*Ft. Worth, Texas*

**BETHEL CHURCH ASSEMBLY OF GOD**

Recently we had Tommy ministering here on a Sunday night. What a glorious time of an uplifting word and transforming preaching. The Word of God presented in a powerful, yet practicable manner. The result was HUNDREDS experienced freedom in His Spirit, thus experiencing the emotion healing power of Jesus Christ.

I gladly recommend Tommy Hawk to any church that hungers to realize by experience the supremacy of God's love. You will rejoice and be encouraged as you watch your people impacted by the love of God that flows through this ministry.

*Ray Lawson, Senior Pastor*
*Redding, CA*

**CALVARY CHAPEL**

Your ministry here at Calvary Chapel, was truly an inspiration. In the fourteen years of ministry, I have never seen a greater move of God than that which we just experienced. IT HAS CHANGED OUR CHURCH.

You as a pastor may call me anytime for the highest recommendation of this man.

*Pastor Brian White*
*Bluffton, IN*

## CHRISTIAN LIFE CENTER CHURCH OF GOD

I am happy to recommend the ministry of Tommy Hawk from Columbus, Ohio. We had the privilege of having him minister to our congregation on a Sunday night. The response in the invitation time was outstanding. Tommy has a strong desire to see unity in the body of Christ through his life and message.

*Dr. David S. Bishop*
*Yakima, Washington*

## LIFE FELLOWSHIP

*Nassau, Bahamas*

Dear Tommy,

Thank you for coming to the Bahamas. Your ministry was a blessing, and of course, you and I will never know the full extent of your coming.

*Pastor Jay Simms*

## FOURSQUARE GOSPEL CHURCH

Tommy has some messages on "Love" that will revolutionize your church; at least it did ours! We are still seeing the results of ministry. The results, lives and marriages in our church healed. His country and western gospel music along with His testimony, "Mafia Freedom" is outstanding. I highly recommend him to you and your church.

*Pastor James E. Sustar*
*Wooster, Ohio*

**REJOICING LIFE BAPTIST CHURCH**

Tommy's ministry of song and messages of God's love has been a real blessing to our fellowship. The Spirit of God in the love of Jesus moved upon our hearts and knitted us together. The reality of Tommy's message of unconditional love brought us assurance of victory in our Christian walks.

*Mike Pangio, Senior Pastor*
*Middleport, OH*

# Roy Nichols

## Nicholsworth Presentations

- Stories, Poetry Recitations,
- Songs (both silly and serious)
- Speaker, Singer,
- Poet, Storyteller

Mr. Nichols appears in kids' programs such as "Dr. Ironbeard."

Appears in adult presentations as self or in first-person as various characters.

In schools, church groups, senior centers, retirement homes, arts festivals & other venues.

Member of: Storytellers of Central Ohio; Buckeye Santa's; Forever Young Theater Group; Vaudvillities Productions; Silvertones; Song weavers

**FOR EVENT SCHEDULING:**

**CALL:** (614) 339-9880

**EMAIL:** Nicholsworth1946@hotmail.com

**WRITE:** 1105 Colony Drive, Box 626

Westerville, OH 43081

# ABOUT THE AUTHOR

Tommy Hawk is an American, founder of Tommy Hawk Ministries, and resident of Columbus, Ohio. He is a Christian minister, author, Bible teacher, evangelist, and former country music artist.

Made in the USA
Monee, IL
25 October 2024